To Jeanne
5-10-24

Copyright © 2024 T.W. Sheffield

Printed in the United States of America

Published by:
Writer's Publishing House
Prescott, AZ 86301

Paperback ISBN: 978-1-64873-490-8
Hardcover ISBN: 978-1-64873-491-5
eBooks ISBN: 978-1-64873-492-2

Cover Design, Project Management, and Book Launch
by Writers Publishing House

I Wore the Wrong Shirt to Work Today

By T.W. Sheffield

Since we are talking about music, here is a song for any aspiring guitarist/singer who may want to give it a try! :) 😊

"Each Other's Eyes" (Key of G)

How would I ever know you	G/Em (2+2=4count)
What could I ever do	Am/D7
I walk down the middle	G/Em
Of the road	Am/D7
Weighing both sides	G/Em
I remembered when I cried	Am/D7
And you put your arms	G/Em
Around me	Am/D7
We both saw each other's eyes	G/Em
And we said our goodbyes	Am/D7
How would I ever live	G/Em
Knowing you were gone	Am/D7
I Love Those Eyes (3X)	Am/C / Am/C / Am/C/G/C

Unless I said goodbye	G/Em
And never looked again	Am/D7
Life is always fair	G/Em
And I never dare	Am/D7
To question what comes next	G/Em
In the middle of the night	Am/D7
Where I always remember you	G/Em
And I cry again	Am/D7
I will never know the end	G/Em
I'll just keep coming back again	Am/D7
I'll never let you go	G/Em
Not even in the end	Am/D7
I Love Those Eyes (3X)	Am/C / Am/C / Am/C/G/C
Someday I will find a smile	G/Em
And my face will come alive	Am/D7
As I move from the night	G/Em
And back into the sunlight	Am/D7
I never stop looking	G/Em

For those eyes	Am/D7
When I stood next to you	G/Em
And I had everything	Am/D7
When I stood next to you	G/Em
And I saw those eyes	Am/D7
This is when I knew	G/Em
I was in heaven again	Am/D7
I Love Those Eyes (3X)	Am/C / Am/C / Am/C/G/C

1

Really?

Imagine ... leaving for work and realizing you are wearing the wrong shirt. But yet where was the right shirt? I hadn't even got out of the garage when I realized the notion. Why didn't I go back inside and change? The right shirt was not in my closet, a nearby store, or anywhere on Earth for that matter.

The problem came to me running away from my mother one day. If recollection is right, I was about four (and I am guessing here since the chronology of my early years is based on geography because this was the first of many addresses). There was a lot of yelling; boy, was she pissed. I just kept circling the table, first this way and then that way, but the longer it lasted, the worse the situation became. At one point, I am sure she caught me, but it was one of many such episodes. The outcomes usually ended in a slap or being tied to a chair. Nevertheless, the occurrence was of such frequency I cannot elaborate since much of the aftermath is locked away in my brain. Avoiding the turmoil became a coping mechanism for me over the years.

The next question becomes, how does this relate to the shirt? Think about it ... A young child is just learning things. Maybe you have a recurring dream. One of being walked out into the unknown on glossy black stones on a pitch-black body of water in the dead of night by a stranger who just promised your mother you would never find your way home again. Then morning comes. You wake to realize it's just a dream. However, climbing out of bed it starts all over. Go ahead ... try to find the right shirt.

In fairness, I was mostly likely difficult to handle, frantic at best. If, in fact, I had been born in the 80s or 90s instead of the 50s, I would have been sitting in the corner drooling from medication. Now, I am not giving my parents a hall pass; it's just an observation. However, as an adult and a parent, both of my children probably survived due to their mother. She carried the coldness required to rule over the household. In our marriage, I held the checkbook with a passion for living. It may seem confusing, but it worked.

Now, with some background context, it's time to pen my story. My plan was to write something regularly that would build a plot filled with stories. I am not

2

writing a biography but a happy, sad, provocative filled with a lifetime of experiences. In the pages to come, you will be drugged through schools, cities, Juanita's marriages, and lovers. All the while, each story will include my friends, drugs, alcohol, fueled rage, and a defeated, sad recovery.

2

World Peace Was Closer ...

... than where I thought I ended up that day when it started. Is that hard to follow? Believe me, I understand. So, take a moment and grasp this little bit of serendipity, which is referred to as a delightful discovery made by pure accident.

One morning, I pulled out of my garage around 4:30 am, leaving Pacifica, CA, and headed to Fullerton, CA. The drive on a normal day took about an eight-hour trip. I threw back a 5-Hour Energy, slid quietly out of the neighborhood, and over to the southbound lanes of Hwy 101. I listened to sports talk ... music ... and psychologists on the radio.

I love this drive, while most thought it boring when you're trying to get somewhere. Actually, I was trying to escape a work day, but no matter, it did not stop my phone from delivering all the messages from the world. I ignored it for long periods and just enjoyed being alone ... untouched ... out of the 'do something now' mode.

Before long, it was time to choose my final fifty-mile route. There were several options in Southern California. All of which pertain to endless freeways and connectors. It's actually amazing and yet somewhat annoying. One route leads to endless traffic, but making a wrong choice might lead to endless traffic once again. So, finally, I settled for the northern loop, with more miles but less chance of heavy traffic.

Finally, once on the 210 freeway, it occurred to me that I was heading to Fullerton, which eventually leads to the 57 freeway, which drops too far south. Then ahead, the highway sign flashes, 'Warning! Warning! Warning! Possible heavy traffic during the backtrack!'

It was time to think quickly; the 605 could work. I recalculated my path and moved across several lanes of traffic. But the change in plan got me on high alert so I would not miss my exit. A few seconds later, the road sign says, 'Rose Hill Cemetery,' next exit. The next thing I knew, my car was heading off the freeway. At the stop sign, a new resolve grabs my attention. It had been twenty-five years since I made this trip. Suddenly, life flashed before my eyes. It is serendipity in its purest form.

The last time I made this trip, it was encouraged by my therapists. In '86, while heading to work on a cold rainy day in December, I was suddenly overtaken with sadness. The feeling arose from a long history of a dysfunctional childhood. But saying *goodbye* was an impossible task at the time.

Only the past has a way of sneaking up and forcing a confrontation. My mother had died six years prior, and I never had the chance to give her a proper goodbye.

She wanted to see me and talk, but I would not listen. I already knew what she wanted, and I did not want to have that talk. Later that evening, she died from breast cancer. Yes, I was there, but way too late. She was gone.

I remember being at the funeral with Dan, sitting next to Jack, and I was surprised he was there. "Keep a stiff upper lip, kids." Let me translate. "We aren't crying here today ... get it?"

Needless to say, I was nowhere near crying. But years later, in the same space at Jack's funeral, his words rang loud and clear. And for the record ... I am patiently awaiting the moment when I make this visit to his gravesite.

As you might discover, the relationship with both my parents was beyond strained. It is one of the most dysfunctional family arrangements that ever existed.

However, it took my mother dying to help me overcome something they helped create. The irony....

On a cold and rainy, miserable day, I decided to visit Juanita's gravesite. Of course, as proclaimed, it was a cluster fuck. After arriving at the cemetery, I could not find the grave. So, after an extensive search, the best option was to ask for help. Needless to say, the office staff came up empty-handed as well. In a bizarre wonderment, we all looked at each other stumped. Then, something occurred to me, as I should have known beforehand. With Juanita's lifestyle, the last name would be different. I gave them her current last name and, behold, victory.

By this time, hours later, all desire to visit her had collapsed. But since we were successful, I better follow through. It might sound funny, but I always carried a beach chair with me. So, in the cold, windy rain, I sat down next to the headstone. It looked like a large chunk of cement. I felt nothing; my demeanor was as cold as the day. So, after a short time, I left. I tried, didn't I?

What are the odds that the next morning, I would wake up really sick? Over the next few days, it got much worse. So, a trip to the doctor became necessary. He walked in and realized I could hardly breathe. "Do you smoke?" He asked. "I try, but it hurts." So, he went on to say that after three days, the nicotine addiction would be gone. And if I smoked again, it would be from a weak will on my part.

To this day, I've never had another cigarette. Juanita reached up from her grave, trying to choke me for not coming to the hospital before she died. In the end, I give her memory credit for my ability to quit smoking.

My next visit to her grave carried more weight than expected. I started with the office staff this time and got directions. Before arriving, I stopped and bought some flowers.

On the way across the cemetery, my eyes wandered, searching for her site. About five minutes later, I saw her marker. It simply stated her name and the fact that everyone called her 'Darling.'

However, the moment I saw Juanita's plaque, my eyes swelled. The tears rolled down my cheeks. I cried, talked, and blew my nose for quite some time. People came and went, but I had no desire to keep a stiff upper lip.

My love for Juanita had been buried for many years, and I was finally able to understand my love was real. Over the years, I missed her dearly. It seems like we miss the people we love the most after they're gone. I felt good about coming this time. In fact, it was this time that allowed me to heal.

The flower hole was filled with dirt, so cleaning it with my hand was impossible. No one had been there for decades. I placed the flowers on the ground and promised never to forget.

Eventually, I dried my eyes and put the beach chair away (before leaving that morning, I had an uncontrollable nudge to put it in my car). Could my subconscious have known? Was it God choosing anonymity? Spooky stuff) The same guy I'd always been grew just a bit more that day.

Jack

In February 1968, I became a juvenile deportee from Junita to Jack. It's interesting to me that I left Jack out of the beginning since he played a major part in my early years. More of Jack will follow later. At seventeen, I asked my probation officer (how I met him in part of another story) if it was possible to leave the county and go live with my father in London. The officer replied that he would release me from probation. He also said if he found out I didn't actually leave, he would have a vendetta for my freedom. Needless to say, I left two weeks later, but not before holding a small party.

The party was held at Juanita's apartment, where I lived. She left us alone downstairs while several of my best friends, including my girlfriend, whom I will never forget, stayed out of control until the early hours. However, it never occurred to me that I might miss any of these people. I was surprised when it happened. Several hours later, I left LAX for my third trip to London

At the end of the terminal in London, Jack was waiting for me. He was not a happy camper. My hair was long. I was wearing corduroys, a white T-shirt, and moccasins. It was difficult to tell if he was afraid of me or I of him. It turned out I was afraid of him. Our conversation was guarded. He said I would need a haircut.

We went shopping at Harrods the next morning, and boy, did I have one of the first-ever juvenile 'do-overs' in history. First, my hair was cut short. I have no words to describe my horror. Next came beautiful suits, shirts, ties, sweaters, a heavy coat, and a fabulous pair of great boots.

The next morning, Jack enrolled me in the American School of London. He wasted no time in getting things squared away. My first class of the day was English. Our teacher was an attractive middle-aged woman who eagerly handed me a copy of 'The House of Seven Gables' and suggested I read it by the next day.

"It will take me a month," I replied.

"You better get started."

Welcome home son ...

Hitch Hiking

At sixteen, we thought hitchhiking in Hollywood and getting rides from weirdos was a thrill. Granted, it is my memory. However, I am sure if something terrifying had happened, it would have been carved into my brain.

Later in life, when I found myself without a car and needed to get somewhere, there was no choice. Although it was relatively safe, if that is what you'd call it, it was still risky. On that note, one time, a guy asked if I was interested in him sexually! OK, that was that creepy! I couldn't get out of the car fast enough.

I asked quickly, "Can you pull over and let me out?". It was in broad daylight. It might have been a different story after dark.

The one issue that happened regularly was getting hassled by the cops. I guess I just had that kind of face.

Each time, it is the same routine, "Who are you, and where are you going?"

They'd run 'warrant checks,' which took forever. In most cases, they were friendly, but occasionally, some were curt – cooperate or go to jail.

One night, hitchhiking home from work, I got let off at a donut shop. It was after 10 pm, and I lived in the local foothills. It was sort of scary, but it is what it is. While standing in front of DK's Donuts with my thumb out, a cop pulled up and, of course, ran me through the paces. He ended up feeling sorry for me and gave me a ride. But I was too afraid to ask if he'd stop at the "Four Corners," where I always waited for a ride under the street lights so I could see who was driving. This cop took me as far as he could, trying to help. But he pulled over in the middle of the night with no moon, let me out in the pitch dark, and headed back to town. Now I was worried. It was a fact that there were weird people on the road; however, since I knew the area, ducking out of sight would not have been hard. Nevertheless, the second concern happened to be that it was summer and rattlesnakes abound. They lay on the roads at night to get warm. Plus, this time of night, not many cars passed except the weirdos, and that had me worried. Now, here is the funny part. An off-duty policeman who lived in the foothills picked me up, was way cool, and dropped me near my house. Go figure.

Reverse hitch-hiking fear. Yes, a real thing. It means when the hitchhiker scares the driver. I was falling asleep while heading home late one night from Marin County (Bay Area) to Laguna Beach in my 1963 VW. So, I spotted these two guys standing by the on-

13

ramp and decided to pick them up and let one of them drive so I could sleep. Wrong. Now, I was worried again; this time, I was pretty sure of my mistake. But you cannot change the rules mid-stream. No matter how easy it would be to pull over and change your mind, ask them to get out. It might not be the second-best decision.

So, I drove ... fully awake and trying to stay focused. They rode with me for several hours before stopping once for coffee. When we got to Santa Barbara, they asked me to get off the freeway and up to their neighborhood. OK ... it was pitch black again, and we were driving where I did not see any cars ... I was certain this decision might be my last.

As my heart pounded, hoping this would be over soon, at the next stop sign, one guy flung the door open and jumped out, with the second following right behind. They disappeared in the darkness. My body wanted to rest, but intuition told me to drive and get the hell out of there. The next day, the engine in my VW blew up ... again ... go figure.

Another kind of reverse fear in hitchhiking is a three-day binge in Santa Barbara before you stick your thumb out. The only thing different was that it was daylight and very hot. I happened to be wearing a long-sleeved shirt. Drug addicts do that. I was tired and irritable and just wanted to be home in my bed. Anyway, this guy, who I cannot even describe, picked me up. Everything was going fine until he exited the freeway and drove to a convenient spot to let me out.

I was shocked. How the fuck was I going to get back to the freeway? And that is exactly how I asked him that question. There was a tense few seconds as we sized each other up ... I was pissed ... he was on full alert. I exited the car ... he drove away, and I walked back to the freeway. That was a rough trip through LA. In fact, I finally called Danny and begged him to come and get me. I was at some Beer Gardens thing ... it felt safe in an unsafe area. He came and got me, and that was that.

The last and final hitch-hiking adventure. I stuck my thumb out and intended to get a few miles up the road. My house was in a little canyon outside of town. A large old, dirty American 2-door sedan pulled over, but before I could understand the situation, one guy got out and ushered me into the back seat between two bad-looking dudes. Something screamed in my head: this was a bad idea. In the back of my mind, there was a dead person recently found beyond the gates at the end of the road. It's presumed to be a murder, but no suspects are ever caught.

If there is a God (your choice ... either God or a coincidence), then to me, what happened next was a God Shot. We came around a corner, and I had never been so glad to see an accident. The highway patrol was parked ten feet from where we were stopped.

I immediately said, "This is where I am going, and I need to get out." The passengers were surprised and said something like, "Really?" I said, "Yes!"

Believe me, I was prepped to start screaming ... they promptly opened the door and let me out.

To this day, it amazes me that I did not share my feelings with the patrol officers; maybe it could have prevented something really bad from happening. Or, it could have put me in real danger. On the other hand, I might have been tripping on paranoia. Guess we will never know for sure. But I almost never accepted a ride from any stranger after that day.

Remembering things

Bobby and I were tight ... at five years old, we both stole cigarettes from our parents. In the backyard, behind his pool, were dressing rooms, so we'd sneak in and puff away. When times were tough ... meaning the peeps got hip and the supply chain dwindled, we took to finding butts on the street and firing them up. Later, it came to our attention, that his sister ratted us out. The punishment restricted us from hanging out for some time, but at that age, it felt like a year.

Bobby was sort of a tough kid for five, and I guess he could have kicked my ass. Glenn was the oldest kid on the block and was a spoiled brat, but he did have cool things. He set up a boxing ring in the vacant lot next door and paired the neighborhood kids by size ... sort of. As I recall, he knocked my older brother flat out, and it was no standing eight count ... it was Gonzo. Next up was me and Bobby. We walked into the ring (I'm guessing we were probably 6 or so) and started flailing away. This was the first time I realized my reflexes were like lightning. Bam ... I smacked him right on the nose before he knew what was coming; blood ran, and so did he, all the way home. Not so tough now, are you, big man. :) No one was more surprised and bummed out than me. I never meant to hurt him.

We used to sit on the grape stake fence in my front yard ... and I kid you not ... we would list the reasons why being a guy kicked ass over being a girl. Remember, we were only 6 years old then. :) Anyway, when things got tough between Bobby and me, I would just climb over my backyard fence and hang out with Glennie. Glennie was a Glennie. Kind of soft but still a little wild. We used to teach the three-year-old kid next door how to cuss at his mother. I have no idea why she never came out and shoved us off the wall. We taught him some words we didn't even understand ... we just knew from older kids that they were bad to the bone.

One day, I was riding my bike home from Glennie's with my roller skates on. Granted, it was not my best decision. Anyway, I was not thinking or watching in front of me. I just rode right into the grill of a parked car and clocked myself. I staggered to my feet, bawling all the way home. The funny part is that I remember hitting the car but nothing afterward.

School #8

In my household, one school per grade was a good average. Then, before long, I was living in Newport Beach, California, attending 8th grade at Horace Ensign Junior High. Junita would just get in a mood and move ... there we went, like three vagabonds on the road again. Oh, yeah, I had (have) a brother, Dan, two years older and a lot different.

We met Mary Lou and Fred, who managed our first apartments after the "Larry" divorce. They had a kid named Randy and we quickly became best of friends. So, Mary Lou and Fred moved from the apartments in La Habra to manage another set in Anaheim, and of course, we followed them. Load-'em up and move 'em out. That was a trippy little town back in 1964 ... not the beach ... not the foothills ... just flat old angry Anaheim. The kids were uptight and thought they surfed ... but they didn't. That apartment lasted one semester, and Mary Lou and Fred were moving again.

By the way ... Randy and I and another guy had been caught smoking at the donut shop by Anaheim High School ... that was rough. The other guy, I can see his face but can't remember his name ... cried ... we were doomed. So, during the semester break, we moved to another apartment complex in Newport Beach. I missed the kids in La Habra; they were reliable and would not fuck with you if you didn't fuck with them. This was not so in Anaheim or Newport ... you had to watch your back ... always.

Somewhere in that first year, Mary Lou and Fred moved again ... and to my surprise, we didn't. I met Mark, another child of a single swinging mother who was definitely a high-wire act. We were great friends and spent a lot of time at the beach with his older brother Rex. He would buy us quart bottles of Coors beer all summer. On the outside of his house was a closet that we used to change clothes, store our surf gear, and drink beer. It was a couple of blocks from 33rd Street and a sweet setup for the summer between the 8th and 9th grades.

Along the way, we ran into some other misguided boys and caused more mischief. We stole, attacked patrons at the nearby Sav-On with squirt guns, and rode our Stingray bikes everywhere all day and all night. Curfew was 10 pm ... again, sweet setup. The summer ended, and Mark was shipped off to live with his father, so we seldom saw each other after that summer. But we did make one last scene that winter.

We broke into Ronnie's grandmother's trailer on New Year's Eve while she was out of town. It was on Coast Highway at Dover. Inside, there was a full bottle of VO. Mark, Ronnie, and I drank a bunch. Mainly Ronnie and me. What a mistake! I haven't drunk brown liquor to this day. After the bottle was empty, we took off on our bikes to a restaurant near Lido Island. As soon as I sat down, everything started to spin, and soon I puked all over the bathroom.

A man walked in and said, "Oh My God!" I made a quick exit.

After five hours of unconsciously puking in some bushes and then waking up at 11:30 pm, it was amazing I survived. My main concern after consciousness kicked in was getting home without being picked up for breaking curfew. Gratefully, I made it home but ran into another scene when Juanita threw me in the shower fully dressed.

Maybe Meds Would Have Been Better

When I started writing these stories, I thought about the very daring, stupid things done as a child and considered keeping the experiences to myself, but somehow, my younger days intrigue me.

Jack took a promotion at work, and Juanita refused to let him commute. We lived just outside of LA, and his new job was in St Louis. Juanita wasn't getting left behind. So, as a warm-up to later years, we all got on a train and moved into a rented house in St. Louis. As a 4-year-old, I thought this was the bomb, so to prepare for the journey, I promptly dressed in my favorite attire. A two-gun Pete pistol belt and a cowboy hat and boots.

Most of what took place during that year and a half is a blur. I do, however, remember watching a lot of Captain Kangaroo. Once, my brother was hiding behind a door watching me catch hell from Jack when I suddenly slammed that door ... and no, I didn't know the dumb fuck was standing back there. He nearly lost the tip of the finger that was in the way. There was plenty of blood, shouting, crying, and possibly a trip to the hospital ... I don't remember. I was busy trying to survive the coming event. Of course, the punishment was worse because even though I didn't mean to hurt Danny it ended up being my temper that took the fall.

We had hay bales in the backyard ... they might have been in the neighbor's backyard, but they were there for bow and arrow practice. Don't ever put a bow and arrow in the hands of children. I am amazed no one suffered a serious injury. But hey ... bike helmets did not exist then, either. We also sledded down streets with cars coming and going, not to mention my walk to friends' houses that seemed to take hours ... yep, I was lost the whole time. Childhood was different back then. Who knew where Juanita was in my absence ... I don't recall her even noticing I was freezing cold and hungry when I got home.

So where am I going tonight ... to the fire! I was striking matches ... they intrigued me probably because they were forbidden ... but I loved them. I'd rip each one from the pack, strike it, wait till it lit, and throw it on the ground. My action was twofold – they didn't burn my hand; however, it was a good way to start fires. All of this happened, and the hay bales caught fire. Now, here's the twist ... I ran straight into the house ... dragging Juanita out to view the situation. She called the fire department to come put the fire out.

It just so happened I was a cool cucumber under pressure. I chose the high road, exposing my guilt to save the neighborhood. OK ... I didn't know it was saving the neighborhood ... that was just a plus ... but it meant taking the responsible path.

After Jack arrived on the scene, my troubles had only just begun. The interrogation started when the top fire guy asked repeatedly how the fire started. I stuck to my story of some big kids starting it and running away, but they eventually wore me down. I was only four ... and copped to the charge.

They actually threatened to take me to jail just before I cracked! Take me to jail ... what for ... being four and stupid? Although I was promised clemency for my plea, I did not receive parole from the belt ... yep ... back then, Dad whipped kids ... and all I could think was, why did I admit it?

So, in the end, St Louis was quite the trip. Dan and I grew up a little and became closer ... Jack and Juanita grew apart a little, which set the stage. Although I was too young to get it, divorce was right around the corner. Jack and Juanita were good people; nevertheless, their marriage was on the rocks.

Shortly after returning to our home on Sunset Drive in Whittier, I was giving guided tours to the neighborhood kids ... down the hall ... pausing ... looking around to clear the coast ... and lifting the painting off the wall so everyone could see the hole my dad made with his fist. It wasn't long before I was sitting on the curb waiting for him to come home ... and you know he never did.

3

The Chess Game

Most teenagers can make friends easily, and I was no exception. So, when I was 17 and moved to London, I met people quickly and started hanging around with them. Steve was cool and played the guitar. I found out later that his father worked for the CIA.

One night, we were chilling on the third floor of their five-story house in Belgrave. His dad was playing the grand piano, the beautiful 'second wife' was somewhere, and the sister and her boyfriend, plus our other friend Richard, were all in the house.

In one of the downstairs floors, a chess game was going on, which soon engaged me. My opponent was Steve's sister's boyfriend, Sebbi. In his mind, he fancied himself as a good player. As a matter of fact, he beat the studious father; no one had mastered him yet. When we started playing, my intention was just to give it my best, but soon he was in trouble.

The family quickly became interested in watching since the game got pretty heated. Nevertheless, I never considered myself a good chess player and certainly had no thought of actually beating him. Although I know enough about chess to know when the game starts to go bad, it only gets worse. Our game slowed as the tension increased. However, I only remember seeing the beginning of the shift, and before long, I was swinging for the head, you might say. So, before long, the harder I pushed, the further away my win became. Maybe that is what made Sebbie so good. Chess is a psychologically driven game, and he was draining my energy.

In most cases, I am not a skilled chess player. Instead, I am a better risk-taker. Looking back, I have no recollection of how the game started and certainly had no strategy. It, apparently, caught him off guard ... a ball-busting bloodbath hit the board. Somewhere along the way, he tried to right his wrong but failed. So, instead of taking the loss, we settled on a stalemate.

Nevertheless, my accomplishment made me proud that afternoon. I played the best, and even Steven's father found the outcome interesting. It was my fifteen minutes of fame. However, my flame of fortune was extinguished along with my chess ego quickly. And indeed, my ego took another beating over the next two years when he beat me probably 200-300 times. Sebbie was my age, a runaway songwriter, a Buddhist of sorts, and just memorizing. Actually, it's brilliant with an emphasis on narcissism. More about Sebbe Cochise Anadia will come later in the rest of the stories.

Flying Upside Down

A normal night usually consisted of pouring the liquor, collecting tips, and then spending them all on drinks. Sometimes, when I was buzzed and wanted to keep the party going, I'd shut down the bar so the chosen ones could stay.

After locking the place up, I darkened the lights, and we slipped into the kitchen and boozed it up until sunrise. However, the drive home was deadly! Not some of my brightest decisions.

It did just so happen to be my night off, and I spent it rolling dice for drinks. When you're hot, you're hot ... since my mojo was good, changing from my preferred drink, Irish Coffee, seemed pointless. As a matter of fact, I won fourteen drinks that night and drank half, then put a marker in the cash drawer for the balance.

At some point, not sure when, I got the brilliant idea of visiting a chick I knew and seeing if she was interested in hanging out with me. I had just traded a little Fiat for a raised VW Baja. To this day, the actual drive to her house is a mystery. After staggering out of the car, I knocked on the door (and I cannot remember her name, but she had very curly, long blond hair and a rough complexion ... and she was sweet)

She answered the door ... took one look at me, and said, "Not tonight, Tommy ... you are hammered."

I am hammered and pissed off now. I jumped back into the buggy and sped away in a fury. How could she brush me off! As soon as I hit the canyon, I punched it. The engine screamed, groaning as I sifted through the gears.

It's funny how some memories just stick with you regardless of the passing years. My Fiat would have sailed through that corner, but not the buggy. I remember it like it just happened ... it literally flew off the ground ... rotated upside down, and slammed into the front end of a parked pickup truck. The sound was enormous, but my only thought was the full tank of gas. Over the next few seconds, while the glass and stuff fell to cover the entire area, I lay there anticipating an explosion.

When it didn't come, I scrambled out the window ... yep, I was that skinny. Somehow, I staggered to Kevin's door. Amazingly, I knew whose vehicle I hit. When he did not answer, to my surprise, I split. I was drunk ... not stupid. No way was I going to explain this to my mother, let alone the cops.

I wandered up the road and remembered another girl who lived in the friendly area. "What do you want?" Jan asked.

"Please open the door," I said, pleading for sympathy, and she opened the door.

We lay on her round water bed and listened to the sirens while the searchers combed the area, looking for some resemblance of me. No way was I going to out myself. When my curiosity overcame me, I recognized a few of the firemen looking for me, and they did sound worried. The night, regardless, was fun. Sometime during the night, I dozed a bit, but the morning light blinded me, peering through the blinds. The pain stayed silent until I tried to get up, but I had to get out and get dressed. I was really hurt and could hardly walk. One of the firemen from the night before passed me on the road and asked how I was.

I said, "OK, how is Kevin's truck and my car?"

He answered, "Car is totaled, and the truck can be fixed."

A friend took me to the hospital that day. They told me nothing was broken and that I smelled like alcohol, so don't ask for painkillers. We headed off to the highway patrol station to get a release on my totaled vehicle. They held me for questioning by the top dawg. He insisted on knowing where I went after the wreck. I said I hit my head and wanted my mother. Then I woke up in the bushes. You are a liar, he screamed. Sign these papers and get out.

It took about a week, but I sold my wrecked Baja Bug and came up with the six hundred dollars so Kevin could fix his truck. I went to work two days later as a walking contusion. Somehow, I lived through the experience but spent the next few months walking or hitchhiking. If that story interests you, keep reading; they only get better.

BB Guns, Birds, Dragonflies, and Neighborhood Girls

Juanita moved us abruptly from our home on Sunset Drive in Whittier, California, to an apartment just off Whittier Blvd. It was the second place I remember living. It was okay at that time. I was too young to figure out her game, which basically left me free to do what I wanted.

Some of the kids made a fort in the area. So, we all hung around. I'm not sure what we did there, actually. As I remember, it was a little crazy. I must have been eight at the time. Shortly after getting settled, it was time to move again. This was a big one to Pocatello, Idaho.

Juanita married Larry, a Buick salesman with two daughters, Mary Jane and Peggy. I was nine, my brother Dan was eleven, Mary Jane was 9, and Peggy was 13. We were the real-life Brady Bunch, however, not like the fun-loving household on the TV show. The tension in the house was scary.

The girl's mother had just died ... don't ask ... I do not know how or why. Juanita was the mean stepmother, and Danny and I were just part of the package.

My nephew, Jerry, had a BB gun that his mother hated, so she gave it to me when we moved. I loved that gun. It became an extension of my arms. It gave me something else to do, and I stayed out of sight. I quickly learned how to draw a bead and compensate for distance and wind. A deadly shot at nine. Dan and I went hunting in a snowstorm, and I bagged my first bird.

The problem was it didn't die ... the distance was too far and I only really stunned it. I was going to finish it off, but the soft-hearted Danny refused to let me. So, he carried it back to the house and made a warm home in a shoe box. But Juanita refused to let it come inside, so he left it on the back porch. In the morning, the bird was gone ... and so was the cat who left its tracks in the snow.

Dan and I could not agree on the gun subject, so we split on that issue, and I became a loner. Before long, I met another kid who had the same gun and keen eye. We spent hours at the pond across the street hunting dragonflies. Nothing like practice to make perfect. The Dads in the neighborhood would take the willing boys pheasant hunting. Our job was to walk out in front and scare the birds, and when they flew, we dropped flat on the ground while the shotguns rattled behind us. I always had my BB gun on these hunts, and I swear that once I hit a low-flying bird, I have no idea what kind, but I heard the BB strike it in midair. Okay ... the bird didn't drop, but I know he remembered me that evening. :)

One dull afternoon after school, I was sitting behind the fence on our back porch with my gun, of course. A group of girls from school were walking up the street next to our house, and I raised that gun and very carefully placed a few BBs across the back of their winter coats. No harm, no foul, but I laughed, and so did they.

I have no idea what happened to that gun. It was a great "cock action" rifle that held about 50 BBs at a time. It had a light-colored wooden stock, with a metal "Daisy" logo printed in gold ink. It is funny, but one afternoon, while we were on a fishing trip somewhere in Idaho, I shot a beautiful Robin Red Breast. Shot it right off a limb, and it was not even a difficult shot. The bird just fell off the limb, dead on impact. Something changed that day, and I felt remorse.

The sadness caught me off guard cause nothing could take back the shot. I'm not sure of the timing, but I believe the gun and I started to part ways. Although my shooting days were not over, they would one day change my love for guns.

Something I Never Understood

Another story that will make you laugh and stay the way I did – confused. It is not important to understand the surrounding circumstances, so this can be done quickly. We were living in Fresno (Juanita, Larry, Mary Jane, Peggy, Dan and me). I am not sure what month it was ... although I know we were there for one school year (5th grade).

We were all going somewhere ... I think it might have been on a vacation or something, and we were all getting in the car. For some reason, Danny was nowhere to be found. We went looking for him and heard this "bang" coming from our bedroom. When we entered, he was standing by the light switch with a large screwdriver in his hand.

He had this "oops, I've been caught" look about him ... slightly tempered with fear.

Wait ... keep reading. For some reason, I still don't understand to this day. Dan took off the light switch and placed a .22 caliber bullet in the wall, only to accidentally touch an electrical wire with the bullet, which caused it to fire. And I swear that is what I heard Danny tell Juanita and Larry.

I heard them ask him (and with a flare of "Are you fucking kidding me ... " in their voices) why?

My mind swirled at this next confession. Whatever he told my parents never made sense, but I think it went along the lines of, "I was trying to hide it."

Really ... hide a bullet in the wall next to electricity? What the fuck for? So, you see, I don't think I heard anything right that morning because it still doesn't make any sense to me today.

We never found the bullet; who knows where it went. Danny put the plate back on the wall and just looked at us from behind his goofy glasses ... revealing the "coke bottle accident" chipped front tooth. I'm here tonight, so I know we must have left that morning ... but I cannot remember anything else about that day.

How To Not Quit

As I stated before, after the car wreck, hitchhiking was my only mode of transportation again. At least I didn't start work until 2 pm ... but getting home at midnight was a trip and a half. It was a sunny day in southern California, and I was standing there with my thumb out ... and the long hair, too. A friendly police officer stopped to see why I wasn't in school. I was twenty-one at the time.

He said, "I will check for warrants, and then you can leave."

"Could you hurry it up?"

"I can make it last all day if you like. He replied.

"No, thanks."

The incident left me getting to work late. And even though my boss was a good guy, he was a hot head. So, when he started yelling at me, I quit. It did not take long to find another job at another print shop. It was a fairly good job, and I was a pretty good cutter/folder operator. The drawback was everyone on the job spoke Spanish. I didn't care, but it bothered them. Each morning, they started saying things to me I could not understand.

When I asked Jessie, who spoke English, what they were saying, he just smiled and said, "They were saying Good morning."

"Okay," I was good with that too.

My next decision also had its problems. I started seeing the owner's daughter. Bad choice ... she was a whack job. In fact, she scared me, and this was before the movie "*Fatal Attraction*" was made. I was living it.

I can't remember her name, but she did not have a place to live, so I let her move into my canyon house. There were some ground rules, mainly staying out of my room. One night, I came home, and she was in my room on my waterbed with someone else. I was not jealous ... just finished. I demanded, "You need to get out now!" She did, and I quit that job soon after.

So, I had a master plan to convert old telephone wire spools into very cool coffee tables and sell them at the swap meet ... perfect. I knew how to build them, and they looked like mushrooms. Here's the problem ... I didn't have a vehicle, and hitchhiking with a three-foot spool table was tough. So, I gave that career up after moving my inventory at liquidation prices ... all two of them!

I am not sure why I was standing on this particular corner one-day hitchhiking, but there I was, and my old hot-headed boss pulled up to the light and said, "What the fuck are you doing?"

"Nothing," I said.

He started about all the work he had and being short-handed, plus how I was doing nothing, and insisted that I come back to work. We cut a deal ... as long as I cut paper and folded it for at least 8 hours a shift, he would never comment on my arrival time again. Done deal ... I needed the rent money.

My scheming continued. It was not something I wanted to direct attention to, but it happened. So here it goes. I knew a bartender who said he was the captain of a purse-saner tuna boat that fished the Ivory Coast of Africa. He invited me to join the crew as a speed boat operator (herding fish!). I was all over that. It would let me get some tattoos, get into some bar fights, and, of course, make money. Money was not a priority back then. I sold everything I had, gave my dog to my brother, and cut my hair. Yep! Cut my hair and updated my passport. Then, I hitched a ride to San Diego to meet the boat. When I walked into their office on their dock, I said I was looking for Tommy, who was the Ship's captain. The guy sitting there laughed out loud. The bartender happened to be on the boat in Florida but was the cook, not the captain. I am certain he told me he was the captain. I asked the guy if he had any other boats I could get on. He laughed again and said the union fishermen across the road would sink his boats if he hired a nonunion guy.

I hitchhiked home and broke into Danny's apartment because he was zoned out and unshakable. As I climbed through the window, I heard his M-1 Carbine engage...oops ... vets are all alike ... a little sketchy.

I simply said, "It's me."

He walked back into his room. So, there I was, nowhere to live, no car, no job, very little money, and wondering what I should do.

You know I went back to the hot head ... endured his joy, "I told you so...."

Life went back to normal work. Like I said, how not to quit endlessly. Oh, it is still going on today ... almost 40 years later.

4

Parts Everywhere, Both Ears and Lost Dobbies

In the spring of '75, sitting poolside next to my new bride, a phone call came for me. Before we got married and rented that apartment, I lived in a small canyon in the foothills with a roommate or two. Tim was one of the roommates. After a couple of years, we all left the house and moved elsewhere. Anyway, the phone call was from Tim, inviting us on a dune buggy trip to the desert with him and his wife. I'd never been in a dune buggy. At first, the idea of driving around in the dirt seemed pointless, but boy, was I in for a surprise.

We met them at their house with our camping gear ready to go. Tim and I were heavy drinkers, but I also loved pot. Neither of the women was interested in these options. It's funny how we even spent time together. We drank and drove for three hours, stopping for piss breaks, when necessary, on our way to what might be called Hell's next-door neighbor.

By the time we got to our campsite, it was already pretty late. We rolled the buggy off the trailer, loaded up the cooler with more beer, grabbed the joints, and were ready to head out. We told the women bye, and off we went. Let's say my first ride would not be my last. We were the fastest thing in the desert. Tim introduced me to the rest of the characters, and we got blitzed.

Tim said let's go to the bar before it closes and get some more beer, and we'll stay out all night. Uh ... OK. We left everyone at the sandhill and started making our way through the whoops and tight turns that headed back to the highway. We crossed the state route and angled up a very rough shoulder of a small asphalt road. At that moment I was having the time of my life ... warm summer night in the desert ... drinking, smoking, and running gas through carburetors ... heaven on earth.

"What say, we see how fast this will go on the asphalt?" Tim smirked.

"Uhhh," was all I could say.

In seconds, we were on the asphalt, at most likely 1:30 am. Tim hit second gear, shifting to third, and then we launched airborne. We ended up in a spin around the pavement. It happened so fast, and my memory has gaps.

"Are you ok?" Tim yelled.

"Yeah, I'm ok, are you?" I shouted back.

Suddenly, we were slipping through the dirt on the driver's side as we heard a road sign snap before we slid to a stop about one foot from a telephone pole. The idea of us hitting that pole still scares me to this day. Once the stun was minimized, I popped my belt and fell on top of Tim. We struggled a bit but crawled out through the roll cage.

Tim looked at me, "Is my ear still there?" as he lifted his hair out of the way. I looked, "Yeah, I think so."

"Well, then, I am ok... You?"

I thought for a second, "Yeah, I'm alive and all good."

The crash must have made some noise because people started showing up to ask questions.

Tim immediately started asking for help to turn the buggy upright, but there was laughter. "Dude.... your gas tank is back on the road, your wheels are bent under the buggy, not to mention the carburetors are MIA, plus the tires are flat."

While Tim stuttered, I reached for a joint to realize they were all gone. They must have fallen out in the crash. It just so happened to be the worst part of the crash...the smoke was gone.

"Do you wanna get your trailer, Tim?" someone asked.

So typical, Tim answered, "No, let's just drag the fucker back."

We did just that. We did get invited to take another ride, but my fun was over ... enough. However, it only got scarier, but that is for another storytime.

In the morning, the girls woke, and we slept. It was the end of a very good time. So, a few weeks later, I bought a sand rail and drove off-road for the last twenty-five years. Never on the asphalt!

I Left in The Middle of The Night

Somewhere along the way, I completely lost it. Yeah, going back to study all the reasons might help, but, in the end, it wouldn't change anything. In reality, the sadness, anger, and confusion festered. It was mostly anger; however, the current events had nothing to do with my reason; it stemmed from within.

Bobby, best friend stateside, mailed me a few "reds" (yep ... mailed drugs right under everyone's nose ... you gotta love 1969 technology). If you are not schooled in street drug lingo, a red is a barbiturate ... in this case, a chemical cocktail that flew by the name of "Seconal." It is prescribed as a sleeping pill, so I took two at 2 am and quietly packed my room with everything I could carry. My addled mind assumed selling my beautiful clothing would help me with money.

Thirty feet away slept my father, his wife, two sisters, and baby brother. It would be the last time I lived under the same roof. Regardless of the reasons, it was terribly sad at that moment, and to this very day remains the saddest moment in my life. So why did I leave? A very good question that there is no answer for. But I got two suitcases and a guitar down a flight of stairs and went through the front door without anyone hearing me.

In my stupor, what happened next is vague, but I believe I got to the train and maybe took a cab. However, the one thing that did stick in my head was the cold. When I arrived at Baker Street, London W1, I joined the Chess Master and his girlfriend. There is no way to explain how this all came about without writing a short novel, probably titled something like, "Dumb Fuck Thought He Knew Everything."

I was still in high school in an American curriculum school, which my father arranged. But I still have no idea what I was thinking. Seriously, I didn't have a clue, so the next morning, I went to school. As I look back, school feels safe and warm, and it helps quelch the fear.

After four or five days, I started to accept my new routine—until my father found me. The principal ordered me to call home, so I refused. Then, she sent me off campus to make the call. Needless to say, I never called home. Instead, I went to the tea house, smoked a cigarette, and went back to school. She found out the next day and was furious. I didn't care what she was.

Years ago, someone I followed told me that my father sat in the swing under the back porch for days after I left. He just stared off at nothing. Actually, in truth, he was feeling what I felt for many years, sitting on the curb waiting for him to come home.

The experience still weighs heavy on my mind to this day, and more could be added, but it doesn't just roll together, at least not for me. However, some things never remained the same; we became friends about ten years later and remained that way for about twenty-five years until his death.

Seasons change ... people don't, a sentiment that has never settled well with me. However, I do believe it is true. My father loved me but resented me for leaving. Stay tuned because I am going to tell you about a meditation that helped me deal with sadness. It's easy, but it might make you cry.

Fat Fucking Freaky Fred ...

The meditation is coming shortly, but there is another story that must come beforehand. So, for now, let me tell you about Fat Fucking Freaky Fred.

Since I loved the canyons, finding another house was right up my alley. I heard of a place on a five-acre ranch. So, as the search goes, later accounts of Fred's wife Jane stated, per a conversation, I had explained being a born-again Christian. I did make a few trips to church via Betty, a girlfriend, but I do not remember saying such a thing.

The other strange part of the story, Fred, was not part of this conversation because he happened to be in jail. If memory serves me right, it was on drug charges. Nevertheless, his Jane was cute and rented me the house.

We moved in quickly, me, my dog, and my horse. The house made a good hideout, as drugs and drinking were still a part of my life. I owned an old VW and had a job, so life was good.

Let me tell you more about Fred. Picture a big guy, 6' tall ... long hair, headbands...jewelry everywhere, and an old gold Cadillac. Did I mention he wore a white Stetson? Although, my memory of him is a bit cluttered since I have known him for thirty-nine years. My earliest memories are some of the best. Stay with me; the stories will jump around. Neither of us worked during the day, so we drank and smoked instead. During the summer of 1972, we attended the sundrenched check dam, where many people gathered to party. There were check dams beyond the gates at the end of the canyon's paved road. Fred was a big guy and carried a lot of weight at this point. He drank white wine by the gallons and floated in a chair that required an inner tube under it to float him, as he always had a gallon jug of white wine tied to the chair on a rope. It stayed very cold at the bottom of the dam and easily retrieved when his glass was empty.

Just the fact no one was seriously injured or killed amazes me. Once, a kid named Billy fell backward off the dam and landed in the rocks 15 feet below.

Everyone held their breath and waited for his response. "I'm OK!" He grinned.

There was broken glass everywhere, dogs of all sorts, cars, young tempers, and eventually, a boatload of drunk drivers heading home.

My old VW spent its life with me, never being serviced. It's not like anyone taught me about maintenance. I never thought twice ... just assumed it would run forever. In the morning, it kept getting harder and harder to start, so I had to pop the clutch. Yes, you can start a stick by pushing it, and when it gets going fast enough, you let go of the clutch, and the car will start.

One day, I was late for work, and the car wouldn't start. It infuriated me (back then, I was furious all the time ... once I ripped my shirt off in anger). Anyway, I needed to get to work. It was stuck in a hole, so pushing it was pointless. I lost it and started throwing boulders at the car. However, I never touched the glass, I just destroyed every other part. After my temper tantrum, Fred and his wife were peeking out the window in disbelief.

I fell to the ground exhausted, then realized what I had done to the car. But, wait ... I opened the door, sat in the driver's seat, and turned the key ... the fucker started right up!

After reality took over once again, the damage started me in the face, and I decided to go see my brother. He was an auto body guy at that point, and I needed his help. Needless to say, the site took him by surprise as well. So, he went to work, and in a couple of hours, it was shaped like a VW again ... one that looked like a wrinkled piece of paper!

A while later, Fred and Jane got into a huge argument. Jane ran out outside, and Fred locked her out. Fred refused to let her in until she grabbed a large boulder. She walked over to his prize possession, but before the boulder took flight, Fred opened the door. Now, who's laughing. :) Fred blamed me for starting the whole boulder thing. Fred also hit a telephone pole while driving druuuunk. He left the car and later blamed it on a deer that caused him to swerve. Fred got sober five years before me.

Smuggling Backwards

My first trip surfing in Baja was fun, crazy, scary, and had a moment of sadness followed by a sense of clarity. We were heading south on Highway 1. It was called "1" because it was the only one that headed south.

We passed straight through Ensenada without evening braking ... that became the rule on every trip I ever took below the border. Keep moving until there was nothing around but country, sweet people, and waves. In fact, at some point, I realized that everything from Ensenada to San Francisco was the same.

We stopped in a small town several clicks below all the confusion and soon learned that the leaders of the pack (brothers) and their friend's needed beer for the weekend ... lots of beer. In fact, the shopkeeper had to put it on a dolly to wheel it out to the trucks. It was a warm day, and I had never been to Mexico or the Baja before. I was totally loving the vibe.

We stopped for gas, and this little Mexican girl, maybe 6 or 7, came up to me with a coat hanger draped with braided bracelets. She held them up and offered to pick one. I do not know if she spoke English, but I pointed to a purple and white one on the hanger, and she handed it to me. It cost a small amount, but I paid her ten times the asking price. I still have it in my Burning Man gear.

Later, we got three of the four trucks stuck in a riverbed ... and I mean really stuck. At one point, we had given up and started thinking about pulling the belongings out in case the tide got high. One of the brothers was sitting in a beach chair ... drinking beers and reading about sexually explicit excerpts from his *Penthouse* magazine. It was a scene.

A local stopped by, had a beer or two, and said he had a tractor. We were encouraged, and Bruce and I took him to get the tractor in the only unstuck vehicle we had. When he appeared following us in a "stolen or borrowed" tractor, which he claimed belonged to a friend of his, everyone started cheering. We were going to give him $100 USD to get us out!

A couple of minutes later, the tractor was stuck with the other three trucks. Oops. So, we went looking for another tractor and found one. However, the two teenagers said they would help but had to get their father. We headed back to update everyone and waited. Eventually, the father and two boys arrived with a tractor that had enormous tires ... at least six feet tall.

He jumped off the tractor, walked out into the riverbed, and jumped up and down.

It liquefied immediately, "Not possible," he stated, and they drove away.

We'd all but given up when another guy showed up with a tractor. This guy was a small dude and a smart dude. He grabbed a huge chain and, one by one, fished them all out while never getting his tractor in the Riverbed. But that's not the really important part of this story. He not only didn't ask for anything, he refused to accept the $100 US. Like I said ... sweet people.

Eventually, we ended up on a beautiful, isolated beach. So, we surfed until late afternoon and pitched our tents. One of the guys opened a jar of peanut butter. Inside was the pot he smuggled into Mexico. I could not believe it—very comical and everyone laughed.

All seven of them hit the tent to smoke their joints. I was the sober member of the group, so I just walked to the cliffs and watched the sunset. The scene struck me with a very lonely feeling, but somehow, it felt awkward, this time feeling sorry for myself again. Then I had a thought ... an epiphany, I guess. I realized that the only way I could feel more alone at that moment would be to walk out of that tent stoned. I was not going back to that kind of loneliness again ... at least not that afternoon.

Ever Wonder What Happened to Them?

Juanita and the rest of us made it one step closer to Southern California, which is where she wanted to be, never mind where the rest of us wanted to be. Yes, Pocatello, Idaho, was nowhere to be, maybe. Unless you were nine years old, skiing, ice skating all winter, and fishing and hunting all summer. My, how I embellish those days!

All I remember is having to move again. I do not remember any talk about it or anything relevant, just that Larry was going to work at another Buick dealership, and we were moving into a new house that would be surrounded by beautiful Fresno, California. The house was cool, and there was a fig tree right smack in the middle of the backyard ... don't ask ... I have no idea why.

I attended an elementary school, 5th grade, as I recall. My teacher's name was, well, never mind. If I mention her by name (and I still remember how to spell it), it will give away her identity, and her grandchildren might sue me for slander. Nevertheless, she was a terrible teacher.

All she did was talk and nothing about learning; although it did not stop her from assigning homework, she never taught one lesson. Plus, she never passed up an opportunity to insult everyone. I guess she was an equal opportunity insulter. Mary Jane got the good teacher next door and evidently learned some things that year.

One of my first crushes was Ginger. Boy, was I hopelessly in love. However, she never knew how I felt. It was my secret love affair. It's a funny thought 'cause meeting people never bothered me, except talking to Ginger.

The first thing that I remember was finishing second in a distance run. I almost beat Jeff. No one ever beat him. He pulled off the win by a whisper. Everyone else seemed happy, but at least I got noticed. Soon, I was a main staple in the slaughter ball game that happened twice a day at recess.

In those days, I went to church a lot. I remember I had a good friend named Richard. It didn't matter to me that he was not part of the "in crowd"; I didn't care. At the time, I was into building models, and it turned out so was he. However, as usual, whenever we started to get comfortable somewhere, Juanita would be unhappy, and we'd have to move again.

Just this memory makes me shrug. So, we packed our things and left for Southern California and remembered that, for some reason, Juanita (from Muskogee, Oklahoma ... the seventh child of seven and apparently spoiled) would not be happy until we got back there.

We landed in Brea, California, in another new house. It was a two-story real home, and the best part was Larry put a swimming pool in the backyard for us ... I loved that guy! I took care of the pool every day before school, and as usual, Mary Jane and I once again ended up in separate classes. This time, I got a good teacher.

So, my friend Richard from the church in Fresno invited me up for a weekend, and Mom let me go. I rode a bus, and his parents picked me up. Our agenda for the weekend escapes me, but it does not matter now.

There are just no memories to recall, but I have a sense that we just did normal things that ten- and eleven-year-old kids do. We had fun, and then it was time to go home.

Later, we planned his bus ride to Brea, and we wrote to each other for a long time. Yes, in those days, we wrote letters. I don't think he had ever left Fresno because the last letter I received was just before his trip to my home, and he signed it ... "come soon." I can remember it like it was five minutes ago.

On my way home from school, right about the same time, Juanita pulled up next to me, shouting, "Get in; we don't live there anymore."

She had moved everything out that day, and we moved into a rented apartment (meaning Juanita, Danny, and me). I have no idea how we could do this. It was like a bad dream. The house was gone, Mary Jane and Peggy were gone, the pool was gone ... everything was gone.

Of course, there were some heavy things to deal with, even in the sixth grade. Never seeing Larry and the girls again, had not yet registered. But that story is for another day. I often think about the people in my past and whatever happened to them. The saddest part was Richard never made the trip to Brea and he never heard from me again. I had no idea how to write about the situation and was way too busy trying to adapt to a new environment (again) and never reached out to him. What was I to say?

Something like, "Uh ... well ... who I was, I'm not ... so see ya later."

Nope ... just never writing again was much easier. I still wonder what happened to him and, worse yet, what he was thinking about my disappearance. What did his parents tell him? It was just another wake in the odyssey by Juanita.

5

Warm Vodka and Strip Clubs

Not long ago, it occurred to me that I am old. It only occurred to me recently (and I'm old) that I always thought I was being sent to spend time with Jack during the summers. The flip side of that coin was that Juanita was sending me off for nearly three months every year. OK ... that might sound like a non-epiphany to you, but when I had that OMG moment a while back, I was dumbfounded. Kind of like when I learned that Jack and Charlotte were going to have a baby. Say what? Oh ... I was 9 years old, and it never crossed my mind that they would need more kids. Weren't Dan and I enough?

Bad parenting in California had kicked in on the second trip to London. By this time, I was fifteen, which just fueled my bchavior. It was another 'Juanita Holiday' with Jack and Charlotte. Jack hooked me up with a job in the mail room at his office to keep me occupied for the summer. It paid 7 British pounds a week (about $21

USD). Many kids my age lived on that amount. In my case, I lived on Jack.

On my previous trip, I met a kid named Patty. We spent much of our free time during the summer roaming the Soho district of west London. We had enough money to be dangerous. At first, we started drinking warm vodka and orange in the pubs where money bought you what you wanted. It was cool because in London at that time it was no big deal and 'Bobby's' didn't care as long as you were peaceful.

But soon, we needed more action, and it just happened the strip clubs were calling out names. OK, neither of us had been officially transformed by a woman. We were stuck on the puppy love of teenage girls' syndrome. So, we made the plunge one Saturday afternoon. It cost us 15 shillings ($2.25 USD), and we were escorted into this dark club. I am not going to lie; it was off the chart. It was no burlesque show, but raw talent on display. We nearly exploded, and everyone there, performers and audience alike was tripping on our youth. To recollection, we looked twelve, but were really 15!

Our adventurous state of mind grew quickly, and we graduated from the day to the night shift. After downing a few warm vodka and oranges we picked our club and paid the entrance fee.

However, our plan fell through the cracks when the bouncer stated, "There are no girls here tonight but, follow me, and I will take you to another club."

So, we looked at each other and hurried to keep up. He led us through the Soho back alleys and pointed down a set of stairs, "Go down, open the door, and go in."

I can say panic set in quickly, but we hurried down the stairs. The blue lights, music, and thick smoke captivated us. After rolling his eyes, the bouncer moved aside, waving us in. I did not look anyone in the eyes as we moved through the crowd. We found two seats at the bar and ordered more vodka and warm orange. It was a mirage of sites, an overstimulating environment, to say the least. We grabbed the drinks and turned towards the stage. The dancer on stage had a rope hanging from the ceiling. Of course, we had never seen anything like what she was doing with the rope. After a few minutes ... maybe it was a few moments ... we turned back to the bar and bought some more vodka ... and, of course, warm oranges. I do not know how much we drank, but the chic on stage was calling us queer boys because our attention was elsewhere besides her. Holy shit ... we were in the mecca of "anything goes" in the bowels of London. I bet we were in danger, too, but that never occurred to our vodka-soaked tiny brains.

I have no idea how long we were there, but I vaguely recall it wasn't that long. We may have been cutting-edge 15-year-old boys, but heavy is heavy, and that place was heavy. We exited to the sound of a communal howl and ended up back on the streets. Once we split, I had to sit down and puke. Then, two Bobby stopped to see if I would live. They laughed at me and said, "Be careful ..." and moved on."... Really ... you're not going to arrest me and call Jack? Oh yeah ... this is London ... not Newport Beach, California.

The summer was far from over. Patty and I were not done. We picked up another friend, Brian, who wanted to hang out with us. Somehow, we concocted a plan. Our decision took us to Soho, where we chose a second-floor red light. They called themselves models. We had enough of strip clubs. It was time to rock our worlds. So, we flipped a coin to see who would ask 'how much' when our choice woman opened her door. Brian lost. We were going to pay her to lay all three of us! We picked a stairway and ascended to the second floor ... took a deep breath, and knocked. A woman in a negligee answered the door and looked at us, most likely in amazement. Patty and I waited for Brian to ask how much. He had frozen.

We both jumped in at the exact moment Brian opened his mouth, and all three of us, in soprano harmony, chirped, "How much?"

I remember this … again so vividly it could have happened yesterday.

She broke her "What the fuck" stare and smiled warmly.

Then she said, and I quote, "You lads will need to come back in a few years," and softly closed the door.

Did we fail? Not really … we just picked the wrong door, and that was that. Needless to say, we left disappointed, horny, and needing some more warm vodka and oranges. You know … even the booze couldn't get us to another door, and soon the summer ran out … the job was over … the money was gone, the strip clubs and Soho became this memory. One that the three of us … who have really never spent any time together since, will ever forget. Patty and I learned how to drink like sailors, and Jack was asleep at the switch.

The "Promised" Meditation for the Sad and Lonely

If you were ever left alone as a young child, girl, or boy, you would understand the emotions that go along with the experience. OK ... here you go. What I am speaking about is when one parent or the other is suddenly gone forever ... by choice ... not by death. The situation happens while the world is still good and you are innocent. After reality sinks in, then and only then, do you start dealing with how to cope with the new understanding. It is from this point that we twist in the wind of abandonment ... at least, that is my experience.

So, this is what took place between Jack (my father), Juanita (my mother, Danny (my older brother), and me. We all twisted in the wind ... some stronger than others and more adept at denial. You could say, wearing your feelings on your shirt sleeve (yes, I was wearing the wrong shirt then, too), and I felt them deeply and often ... at first. Gradually, life found a rhythm again, and we all moved on. Jack remarried and started a new family. Juanita remarried and continued the insane odyssey. Danny was always a loner, and I developed the fine art of deception.

Meditation only works if you've lived through everything life throws your way ... both good and bad ... and are still reaching for closure on a moment of clarity you experienced so many years before. Believe me, it does not help even though you might be 'fine' with everything. I like to think of the word "fine" as an acronym ... Fucked-up, Insecure, Neurotic & Emotional. Being FINE with this type of loss smacks with denial, not acceptance. Here is where we all scatter with different takes on life. I chose to spend way too much money on therapy ... and then I found this meditation on a $5.00 audio tape. The guy's name was Bradshaw ... but who cares?

Read this, and then take a break and give this meditation a try. Close your eyes in a quiet place, and meditate if you can. When at peace and calm, turn your memories back to the earliest moments in your life that you can see in your mind's eye from your memories of when everything was still OK. Picture the home you lived in, walk out to the front yard and, look at it, see every detail you can remember. Look at the roof line, the windows, the vegetation, and the garage door. Next, look down at your tiny body to see what you are wearing. Absorb that vision.

Now ... walk to the front porch and look at the door. My driveway was curved around the front lawn. My door was a light mocha brown with those square wooden pains and a brass knocker. The porch was distressed brick. Standing there in my black and white striped swim trunks, I reached up and gently knocked on the door. You can do the same thing. Just take your time and really create the way it was ... outside and inside ... feel the moment and be open for anything.

You hear someone coming but expect to see one of your parents. Instead, the doorknob turns, and you recognize the squeak. However, the expectation is anything other than what's anticipated. Your eyes are focused on the floor, amazed by the size of your feet. Then, seconds later, the memory is halted when another pair of feet are standing in front of you. Something is very familiar about the sight, so you slowly look up and then you realize the person standing in front of you is actually "you" all grown up. It surprises you, but the atmosphere is filled with love. The adult 'you' picks the 'child' you up and hugs you while saying they love you. After crying, the meditation is over.

The lesson was not meant to blame anyone. Sometimes, the things we accomplish seem effortless because they happen at a very young age. We learned to cope. Is our 'coper' broken? "Yes," as I was told many years ago. I learned that living through everything helped me cope. It's not resilience; nevertheless, some make it, and some do not. Someone once told me that seasons change; people don't. Maybe they were wrong.

Christmas On Top ...

I concluded, after surviving my childhood, that being alone was not a good thing. I decided it was time to just spend my time around people. It didn't take long for my plan to succeed.

One year, Linda, a young girl my age, latched on to me, "Do you want to get the hell out of dodge?" I asked.

"Yes, that'd be swell...I know a great place where we can maybe find a house and chill."

We jumped into the car and headed for the canyon. The first stop was a local real estate office; however, it was 1971, and my hair was two years longer, and I was buzzed on pot. Needless to say, we walked out empty-handed. Really? Next stop, back down the hill to the Tasty Freeze to buy a newspaper.

Bingo ... house for rent in the canyon. We called, and a woman answered, "Hey, I am calling about the house?"

"You can buy it for $17,000 or rent for $225.00 a month. It's vacant, she said.

"We'll take it." Hindsight, we should have bought it.

The house was a two stories cliff-hanging gold medallion electric place. We moved in and brought another couple looking for an escape as well. Both girls I knew from school; George was older... just released from the Marines after a tour in Vietnam. Our paradise did not last long. The girls ended up hating us, but the two of us got along great. However, at the time, I had no idea how self-destructive the time would become. We stayed stoned 24/7. But we were into some pretty heavy patterns that led both of us off the map.

Well, Linda ran into some inheritance and left to become a dancer in Las Vegas. The other girl, Judy, got disgusted with our lifestyle and split. George left shortly thereafter; he was just done ... too much Vietnam and everything else. There I sat with a new puppy dog (Beethoven), a huge house and no one else around. I was new to the area and too young to drink in the bars.

Somehow, I met a guy who sold pot ... they were easy to find back then ... in fact, this guy was a pilot and flew the corridor between Mexico and the US desert ... let's say he was an importer of sorts. He had a roommate who visited my house and offered to move in. Neither of us was interested in the dealer's thing. My new roommate was an artist and tripped out the house. We got along pretty well at first, but he was 5 years older and kind of an authority figure ... not a good thing for me and my temper. Soon, a fight broke out; fortunately, my wrestling skills saved me again. I couldn't finish him off, but he was stuck in one of my holds that always led to a stalemate. Not long after that, he brought another roommate home from work. It got confusing in a hurry, and it was time to find another place to live. But this time, I was staying in the canyon.

It did not take long before I found a small house in the upper Shady Brook neighborhood. However, the owner was gay and a manipulator. I wanted nothing to do with him or his lifestyle. Another guy, Phil, who lived in the canyon with his father, walked in and said I am going to take the second bedroom. I said OK. He moved in, paid half the rent, turned my dog (Beethoven) into a fighter. He became one of my best friends ever, but our situation with the owner got too strange, and we moved.

After our weird encounter with that landlord, Phil and I ended up on a street called Olive Drive. He knew the area well, having grown up on that street. As a matter of fact, he showed me a tunnel through the thicket behind the house he made growing up. Once you exited the other end, it was clear sailing to the top overlooking the south wall of the canyon. It was a couple of thousand feet up and very beautiful. Very quiet.

Beethoven and I made many trips to the top ... he flushed the snakes and ran like the wind ... he was an athlete for sure. I did not realize until that moment, which is a shame, but I really loved that animal with all my heart.

Christmas that year was especially appealing because I was on my own. Jack went to London ... Juanita was in Hawaii ... Dan was in Vietnam. There was no tree ... no presents or dinner ... just me ... the dog ... the wine ... and the pot. I packed a few things ... a large blanket ... some munchies ... the wine ... the pot. Then Beethoven and I headed to the top. It was one of those California Christmas days ... bright, deep blue, brisk, sunny, and crystal clear.

On the top, the mustard weed was 6 feet tall and bending with the wind, so we pushed our way to the middle and laid the blanket out, crushing the weeds. We were completely hidden, and it was beautiful. I ate ... I drank the wine ... I smoked the pot ... I read a book ... slept off and on in the warm sun ... Beethoven roamed and guarded us all day long. It turned out that Christmas alone was more than "not so bad." I will never, ever forget that day, the warm sun, and I loved it. The connection with Beethoven is something I will cherish to the grave.

At Gun Point

Well ... once I made a random trip to the Red Rock desert down in Arizona with this friend named Bruce. We were stoner buddies, and the year was 1971. I was living in a very cool place in Laguna Beach at the time and going to night school, so Jack would keep sending the $220-a-month child support (I never did know where he came up with $220, but that was what it was).

Bruce and I drove to Arizona; the reason escaped me. We drove around from one place to another, but I met quite a few people, and of course ... because it was "back in the day," they were all pretty cool. We shared a lot in common, or at least I thought we did.

You see ... there were people back then who were enamored with the easy money made from drug dealing ... and I was not one of them. The trade-off never seemed worth having the money to pretend to be someone else. To me, just having money never meant anything except you had money ... period.

I totally remembered this one couple ... they were cool, and we partied with them (partying simply means we got stoned and/or drunk). We partied with quite a few people over the two days we were there. Bruce was married, but that didn't seem to matter because he had this girl down there. Eventually, I realized why we were down there ... so he could bang her. I was very naive back then. Either way, I was having fun, so that was that. I kept telling everyone to come visit my house in California.

Eventually, we made it back and Bruce dropped me at my house. A few days later, my roommate and I were BBQing in our backyard. We had a few beers when the doorbell rang. When I opened the door, it was a guy named Frank from Arizona. He brought a friend, so we drank some beers and relaxed. Frank was a large man ... recently released from the Navy ... kind of nice with a scary sort of overtone.

He asked, "Have you seen Mark and Stacy?"

I said, "No ... why?" Apparently, they ran off with a large amount of Frank's weed and his money. "Wow," I said ... like who cares ... surely not Brent and me.

They were on a road trip searching for them, and since I'd been inviting people to my house, it was the first stop.

I didn't give it a second thought ... until the doorbell rang again. Frank looked out the window and pulled this big fucking gun out of his pocket, "Open the door!"

Brent and I both spaced out ... what the fuck was this?

So, I opened the door, Mark and Stacy came in all smiles ... until Frank stuck his gun against Mark's head.

"Whoa ... wait a minute," I said ... "not here."

"Take a walk; we'll be gone when you get back," Frank shouted.

Since I didn't have a gun ... and calling the cops was out of the question ... Brent and I left after giving them final instruction, "don't do anything nothing here ... leave ... and

lock the door behind you."

So, how do you deal with that? I was totally freaked out ... so was my friend. Plus, he was not happy with the friends I made in Arizona. Like I told him, how could you figure that I would meet these people and that both parties would come to my house, one hiding out and the other looking for them?

It's just crazy ... and so were all of them. We returned shortly, and they were gone. The next day, we learned they took the two back to a motel or house or someplace in Costa Mesa and had the girl call her mom and ask for a large sum of money. Of course, she wasn't supposed to call the police, but of course she did.

So, the mom shows up ... knocks on the front door ... it opens, and POW ... the cops come out of the bushes ... run in, and subdue everyone without a fight.

Results ... the cops took all of the dope ... the couple got arrested for possession with the intent to sell ... Frank and his friend got some violence charges ... but who really cares, aye?

What I cared about was the phone call from the FBI, wanting to know everything. I told it like it was ... both parties showed up at the same time ... and the rest is history. They wrote it down and left and never called again.

I never heard from or about any of those crazy people again. Nor did I travel with Bruce again either!!!

The Early Hours of the Morning

It is the early hours of each morning when I wake alone.
I lay in bed and stare out into the darkness
I remember so many parts of my life as I daze
Some of them are horrible and make me sad
Others are wonderful and make me smile
But deep down inside my consciousness, I know
That much too much has caused my sadness
I never get through a morning wakening anymore
Without a torrent of grief and remorse of times gone by
I never cry because I do not know how
I want to open the floodgates and beg forgiveness
I want to weep deeply and acknowledge my past
I want to embrace my goodness and be loved
And still, I just put my feet on the floor
And walk straight into another day of the unknown
I will someday wake to closed eyes, with the grief gone
Is there something beyond life that we all see someday?
I do not know, but I will someday never know again
Never see the sunrise again
Never see the sunset again
Never hold the ones I love again
Never know a single thing again

I will have done my best

I will never rest

And I will never be missed for long

6

Strawberries and Horses

Two of the most wonderful events in my life were introduced to me by my roommate. Something that never occurred in my circle. The Strawberry Festival and the Horse Auction. It's amazing how these events could come together and create so much joy. I cannot tell you how this next story came to fruition, but one afternoon, my roommate came home and walked into the house with two beautiful girls as if it were nothing.

"Ey, Chuck, what's up?"

"Well, I met these two girls at the Strawberry Festival, and they came home to hang out."

"Okay," I was not going to argue.

Nevertheless, I was still mourning the loss of my former girlfriend. Who apparently went dancing in Las Vegas and never came back. However, my sorrow quickly dissipated after taking one look at Rachel. She was a fox with a great body and a killer smile.

We hung out all afternoon and got to know each other. As it turned out, Rachel and Monique were runaways. So, we did the right thing; we allowed them to stay and spend the weekend. We did the second right thing and took them home. When we got to Rachel's home, I was expecting a lack of parenting. Some disinterested parents could care less about their kids. My Upbringing really played a part in much of my thinking in those days.

By the way ... Rachel was actually Connie. Her dad was a young-looking, silver-haired guy who drove an orange Road Runner. Connie and her mom looked a lot alike, but her mom was still the bomb. They were actually okay with me bringing Connie home and asked if we wanted to go to the horse auction with them. They managed a horse stable as a part-time thing in the oil fields overlooking Huntington Beach, and the auction was an outing for them.

A few days after we met, we headed for the Horse Auction. After agreeing to go, I instantly became Connie's boyfriend. Since I am, however, a compulsive guy, I leaped from just knowing them to wanting a horse in a few seconds. So, before we left, I got some cash.

As we watched the horses come in and out, all I remember was the auctioneer yelling, "Sold to the young fellow in the back."

I had bought a 17-hand retired Thoroughbred from Utah that was acting fairly wild.

Connie's Dad, Dusty, replied, "You can keep him at our stables, but you have to get him there."

I remember going from person to person, looking for someone with a horse trailer. Since no one accepted, I hitchhiked with the horse. And eventually got a ride.

The next day, everyone at the barn watched me ride the tall beast. So, I swallowed hard and climbed on bareback. The anticipation of expecting him to erupt never happened. He stayed calm, and we just walked around with no problems. So, we embarked on a really good summer. Connie and I rode almost daily and often on the beach. I rode Connie at night. :) The joy I talked about was brought on by Connie and the horse, and I loved them both. We had great plans. But the cool part is I've never experienced a horse like this one. My only other encounter with a horse was at a rented stable. It seemed a natural fit for me to ride horses over the next few years. I rode several but only owned the first one from the auction. I got along with them all. Connie had a Pinto, and the two horses got along well.

Nevertheless, my story about horses could go on for quite some time about the places we went and the things we were planning on doing. For some reason, I decided to move my horse to a ranch in the foothills where I lived. I lost Connie in the process. We never saw each other again. As I sit here writing this story, I still miss her. Like many of my other memories, much is blurry.

What I do remember is that two or three years later, Monique (she was the other girl from the Strawberry Festival named Jan!) walked into the canyon bar I was tending and sat down looking incredible. Before the bar closed, she asked to stay the night. So, come for a drink and stay awhile. In the end, we were not for each other. I took her home the next day and never saw her again.

So, to this day, I am a horse person. To this day, I love those two girls. To this day, I am grateful for the memory. To this day, I love strawberries and horses.

Never Content

At some point, the factory job ended. I finally walked out and stopped at the neighborhood bar for a beer on the way home. When I first moved to the canyon, I was not old enough to drink and the locals were not very nice ... more like old and crabby ... they literally stared us out of the bar when we stopped for a drink.

However, one night, we were surprised. A new owner took over, and when we walked in, he smiled and offered me a beer. So, I took the chance to ask for a job. But, since I am a smart ass, it was said with tongue and cheek.

He looked at me, "Well if my current bartender calls in sick again, I will call you."

I gave him my number. Later that evening, the phone rang. "Hey, this is Bernie. I own the bar. I will make you a deal?"

"Okay, what deal?"

"If you cut your hair, trim the mustache, and preferably wear a clean shirt and tie, I would give you the job. It's $3 an hr. plus tips." (Hey, it was 1973. Rent was thirty a month).

I called the local beautician, bought a tie, and got ready to go. "Red" was the chef, a good one but a complete drunken screwball. After the bar closed, he was drunk every night. On the weekends we had live music and dancing. Red also happened to be a good bartender, so he taught me quickly. Plus, my girlfriend was a cocktail waitress, so she quizzed me for hours on the drinks and ingredients. Bingo, one week, I was a rockstar bartender.

On the weekends, we had two or three waitresses in the dining room and a long bar with about fifteen seats. The tables in the bar held another fifteen or twenty people. Once my feet got wet, the owner let me run the place myself on the weekends. No bar boy and no help. The waitresses and the clients loved me. Oh yeah ... and I really over poured ... maybe that's why they loved me. :)

The place always lost money, Monday – Thursday over the years. Bernie did have a plan. He hired me, a local, and I attracted the local kids that otherwise weren't coming in. Red made cheap dinner specials during the week ... we rocked it. All was good, and this is where I learned that liquor was quicker ... and the cops didn't care ... and I could drink with Jack.

What does this all have to do with "Never Content?" Well, I have never been content (and always wear the wrong shirt). And although life was OK ... I was not. I needed someone who could make me whole, and then, one night, she walked in. She became my new waitress for private parties on Monday through Thursday. We held these for the locals.

But, back to the waitress. Her name was Lauren. She was incredible, from the south, and I never imagined she might like me. On slow nights, we'd drink and laugh, then close the joint. I'd even occasionally drive her home.

Not long after my heart fell in love, her boyfriend Charles flew out to bring her home. Of course, he was tall, dark, and handsome. They appeared to be a great couple. At the time, I was not thinking about her ... not as a lover. So, Charles packed her things and flew home. While we drank and talked that night, apparently, she told her boyfriend she'd follow in a few days. I gave her a ride home. When I pulled up to her house and I said good night ... she leaned over and laid an amazing kiss on me. I was dumbstruck and, of course, instantly in love.

Why she never followed Charles home was none of my business ... why she hung out with me was none of my business ... and in the end, when she left with her girlfriend to go to Hawaii for some fun, it was none of my business. So, you see ... I was content ... then I was in love ... then I was alone ... then I was not content ... then someone else came along, and then I was content again ... and on and on it goes!

I saw her one more time several months later at a party. I told her I was getting married in two days, and I was! I kissed her, she kissed me back, smiled, and said, "I'll see you after the divorce." Another broken heart.

Bent Trip

Yes, I know there is no such thing as a "bent trip," ... but that is what Richard called it (and it might have been what I called my first drug experience ... I cannot really remember the author at this point!). I had been in London for a few months and hooked up with Steve, a guitarist from my school. He was connected with Richard who said he had the bent trip and who used to go to the same school Steve and I did ... I think. Anyway ... looking back on it he was a true musician. The guitarist was sort of a crowd guy and surely interested in looking good anyway. The two of them were trying to put a band together. They played guitars, and a Welsh kid had a drum set. I wanted to be in the band too. They needed a bass player ... and I thought ... how hard can that be?

Jack bellied up to the music bar and bought me a Vox Wyman Teardrop Bass and an amp (man, do I wish I had that rig back!). The others had already been teaching me the guitar, and now they concentrated on the scales. I had no idea what music was, how it was written, what notes went together, or anything else. But how hard could it be?

Teach me the notes in a key ... tell me what key you are in, and I'll create rhythm (oh yeah ... FYI ... I was tone deft and could not keep a beat ... pretty fucking funny, hey). One thing I learned later ... there is a melody somewhere in a song that needs to be followed if you are playing with other people ... way beyond notes in a key played randomly. Now you should have the picture ... yes?

There was one song we did that went on for as long as we wanted—and it did have a "hook." It was called "Destiny and Company." The other guys dreamed up a song about forsaking everything to play music ... and that was their influence. Steve's influence was the Merlin Wizard's robe he wore and the screeching guitar that he created with a slide and a distortion amp. Richard, Pepper, and I were to keep the bottom end together while Steve wandered through his limited screeching scales. Richard actually taught me a 4-note riff that included 6 beats. To this day, it amazes me how that simple riff worked with everything they were doing. I was officially an up-and-coming bass player ... I had 4 notes mastered in a song.

So, here's the deal ... Richard hooked us up with a gig at an English school ... we were the first band up for their dance. I am kind of foggy on all of this because

1) ... I was not a musician, and 2) ... I was not a musician, and finally, because I was a little stoned and completely freaked out. The next problem came about when I purchased some hash we were going to smoke, and we kept it at Richards. We ... Steve and I got this panicked Richard on the phone at about 3 pm on gig day. He is completely out of his head ... he had smoked some of the hash ... it was his first time ever to be in an altered state of mind ... and remembering my first time, I completely understood what he was going through. But what the fuck Richard ... why today.

He was almost hysterical when he uttered, and I quote, "I am on a bent trip."

"No, Richard, that is a "bad trip," and you can't actually trip on pot."

We were down one guitar, the only real musician among us—the author of the only song we knew—and we're going to play it with Pepper. It's our first time ... ever ... in an auditorium in front of English school kids, we do not know from Adam. OK ... let's do it!

We loaded our gear onto a bus and dragged it all to the school from the bus stop. Steve busied himself with the setup ... his thing ... we sort of tuned up and got ready to launch our careers. I should stop ... this is getting long, but you have to hear the ending!!! We thrust into the song. Steve actually sang pretty well. I couldn't hear Pepper over the noise, so I had to concentrate on playing the same 4 notes in a 6-note pattern over and over and over. I see Steve from time to time ... he is jumping all over the place in his Merlin robe. Then he abandoned the lyrical parts of the song and fell completely off the edge in what ended up being the first-ever 40-minute guitar solo with a drummer and bass player who are not even on the same planet. It had to have been horrible, and I also noticed the kids had stopped trying to dance (this was a dance) and were becoming unsettled.

Fortunately, there was another band that came on after us ... but the crowd had gotten nasty anyway. We quickly tore down ... meaning we grabbed everything we owned, drug it all out the back door, and ran. I am not kidding when I say I ran ... to the bus stop and prayed that one would come quickly. Once we were safely on the bus, we started laughing ... sort of gallows laughs ... but we missed the hanging.

Of Richard, I have no memory of his take on our outing. I know that was our only gig. We all consumed the smoke ... which had been a "California ... let's get stoned for the gig" thought that I should not have followed through on. I am fairly certain that Richard never tried it again ... one "bent trip" was enough.

Later on, I hung out with Steve, who helped me help Sebbe with his music. Steve's sister became Dihilo, Sebbie's girlfriend. Pepper disappeared forever ... Richard is still a well-known musician, as I write this story.

Looking Thru The Bottom Of The Glass / Key of D
Feb 26, 2024

I was sitting at a / bar one night	D/G (4count)
Looking thru the / bottom of my glass	D/G (4count)
When she came over and asked	A (4count)
If I'd be around / for a while	D/G (2count)
Didn't know / what to say	D/G (2count)
So I just said / I didn't / know	A/G/D (12count)
Then she set down / next to me	D/G (4count)
Her eyes were as pretty / as they could be	D/G (4count)
I smiled at her and noticed	A (4count)
She were as free / as a bird	D/G (2count)
As free as a bird / just like me	D/G (2count)
As free as a bird / gliding thru / the sky	A/G/D (12count)
We shared stories / drinking that bar closed	D/G (4count)
We walked out under / the fluorescent lights	D/G (4count)
And we held each other close	A (4count)
It was as though we were / old friends	D/G (2count)
Like we knew where we had / been	D/G (2count)
Hoping / we'd find each other / again	A/G/D (12count)

I watched her walk / away in the dark	D/G (4count)
Still hoping / she would be back again	D/G (4count)
I know there is no way of knowing	A (4count)
If we'll ever see / each other again	D/G (2count)
I will look for her / every day	D/G (2count)
I will dream of her / every night	A/G/D (12count)
I wish she would be / at that bar again	D/G (4count)
Where I'd find her / waiting for me	D/G (4count)
Her smile would say everything	A (4count)
I would look at her / and remember	D/G. (2count)
Ever memory we / had shared	D/G (2count)
I saw it all / thru that glass / on the bar	A/G/D (12count)

Bellamy's

I am not saying anything derogatory about the two narcotics officers who frequented this establishment. It stays open late at night and always attracts the kind of young people that get their cars searched. Often without reason. It was, after all, the summer of 1967 in Newport Beach, California. Rumor had it that they kept a great deal of what they confiscated. I am willing to bet that was bad information from those who got caught holding. Nevertheless, it was a game of cat and mouse for sure ... and the stakes were relatively high.

At that time, I was associated with a tough crowd. A few of these people were trying to be heavy drug dealers ... most of them were just the usual Joe's on the street. One in particular that I have never forgotten and can actually still see his face in my mind's eye 45 years later wore a "wire." Over time, pondering the incident, the coincidences became too obvious. Have you ever just barely survived a very bad experience ... one that caused you to shudder upon reflection?

Well, as Jimmy Hendrix once said ... "I have."

At 16, we all do our best to be cool. I walked away from sports and minimized school importance, just focusing on my network of friends. So, somehow, I knew these people in the auto body repair business ... and let's just say the paint must have affected them. They were all much older—can you say decades? The guy who was wearing the wire for the police was one of these guys.

"Hey, do you want to earn some extra money?"

"Of course."

"It would require you to do whatever I need."

I'm speaking about the work in his shop. I was not a criminal ... not, then ... not now ... never was ... so his inference went over my teeny bop head.

"Doing what?" I looked at the clock.

"I need you to pick up a client's car and bring it to the shop."

"When?"

"10 at night. You have nothing to worry about. Plus, you wanted the extra money."

"OK!" He sucked me in.

When he picked me up, we cruised through an expensive neighborhood on the bluff.

I got nervous because he was jumpy. "Hey, you misunderstood my statement about doing anything for money. Working in the shop is one thing, but this is not work. and please take me home immediately." I can say that was that.

There is no doubt in my mind I would have been arrested for Grand Theft Auto. The guy was way over his head in helping get people arrested. So, if the other people should have been arrested, it was between them. At the time, I was a pot-smoking moron in the wrong place at the wrong time. But I guess smart enough to say no....

A few days later, I was caught red-handed with pot, and the cop quoted something I told the 'wire guy' in confidence. The next few weeks were rough, but I was determined to right the ship ... that's when I called Jack. Dad, you always wanted me to come live with you ... and now would be a good time if that is possible. Jack was a lot of things ... neglectful was not one of them ... reliable was one of them. I was on an airplane and out of that environment almost instantly.

So where was Juanita during all of this trouble I was getting into? She was busy drinking with her boyfriends, who threw money at me to go have some fun. I should have returned the money ... in an uncomfortable manner ... but I was in too deep to see the truth.

Jack and I never "righted" the ship, but we tried ... I swear I would be dead or worse today if he hadn't cared enough to send me a ticket into his world. It may have taken a while, but it changed my life forever.

Bad Flight

Life has a way of making us contemplate our actions. In my younger years, there were some scary things, and I have yet to be honest about my drug and alcohol battles. So, what will it be tonight? Well, I already know 'cause I wrote the title. Suddenly, surfing re-entered my life. Since my son and neighbor dragged me back into the water. If I left Bret's mother out of this picture, it would only be because I chose to ignore her roundabout influence. When he was young ... 9 or 10, I guess she always took him and his buds to the beach during the summer; they would stay all day. Bret would never come out of the water. According to his mom, he got out of the water ... climbed back in the van ... ate his sandwich, and went to sleep for the ride home.

After Bruce and I started surfing hard, we made several trips to Baja. We often took a few of the kids. It was a good time back then, and nothing bad ever happened. But soon, that was not enough ... so one day I picked up this flier at the surf shop ... just for a goof and handed it to Bruce. The next thing I was in a 6-seat low-wing piper with Bruce, Bret the pilot, and two people we just met. The crazy pilot had overbooked the flight to

Isla Magdalena on the southwest coast of Baja ... and we flew a day late due to the weather.

Forget the time on the island ... suffice to say we had a good time ... caught some waves ... camped under the stars ... made some lifelong friends and managed to live through it all. There are stories inside of stories revolving around this trip ... but let me focus on tonight's tale.

When we piled back into the airplane, it was pouring ... we were kind of low on fuel, and we took off anyway. At a certain point, the pilot said we were going back ... we couldn't make it in the weather. On the way back, he saw the highway below and had an idea ... oh no ... this sounded bad. He decided he could follow the highway to the mountains (they were 6,000 feet high, if I remember correctly) and go up to 8,000 feet and "triangulate" for position and course. What the fuck was triangulate?

The headwinds over the mountains had to have been 30 mph or greater ... the rain was coming down so hard you could not see out of the windshield ... we were stuffed in this tiny shell catapulting across the peninsula while the pilot was chain smoking out the wind wing ... holy shit ... if we crash and Bret dies, his mother is going to dig me up and kill me again.

And suddenly, this Mexican-accented English came out of the radio, "What are you doing up there?"

"We are heading for Loretto Bay," answered the pilot.

"Are you crazy," answered the voice ... I am not kidding ... that is exactly what he said ... and I have to agree.

"Report back in 5 minutes ... out."

"So, a few minutes later, the voice returned and, sort of panicking, reminded the pilot that he was supposed to report back.

"Okay, sorry," the pilot replied.

I did not really pay attention to the guy at the stick, but he had to have been struggling to stay on course. FYI ... triangulating means using three beacon signals to figure out your position. He had maps on his lap. So, we are all looking out ... trying to find something other than rain and clouds ... and here is the most amazing thing ... all of a sudden, there is a hole in the clouds below us, and we all saw the breakwater and boats and land. The pilot dropped the plane in an exaggerated descent before popping out below the clouds. There was the airfield, the base of the mountains we had just crossed in heavy headwinds, zero visibility, and pouring rain.

The pilot took heavy Mexican authority abuse about his stupidity and was asked to stay on the ground until the weather cleared ... we left anyway. And while fueling the plane, we learned that we had actually landed on fumes ... it was that close. We took off and flew for four hours at about 200 feet altitude just over the beaches of east Baja, straight into Brown Airfield just outside of San Diego, where we began the trip. The airplane looked like a well-lived VW Micro Bus.

When we left that morning, on our way to the airfield, we were wondering who else would fly to southern Baja in a rain storm. But, after arriving, there was this guy and his son standing in the rain holding their surfboards and duffel bags ... that must be them. Soon to be best of friends and make many more trips with us ... or us with them!

7

Abandoned

My friend Bruce, who has been trying to drown me since he got me back in the water 20-some years ago, decided it was time to try again. The 'Bad Flight' was a precursor to a fifteen-hour jet flight to a remote island off of Fiji. FYI ... this is not the home of the 'Endless Summer' wave that goes on (shoulder-high mushy) for miles. It is the home of the Pacific outer reef break that sucks up water and pitches when it slams into the reef shelf. Once it goes over your head, you had better be a very good waterman, or things might get bad.

The stage is set ... we are heading for an exciting place ... Bruce, Bret (my son), Mel, and Drew (his son). The boys are fifteen and sixteen. Both were on the low-wing piper when we almost died in Mexico. They were pumped, but it was a long flight, so we napped in the Hawaiian airport. Thank goodness for Excedrin PM. It worked well for about eight hours.

Upon our arrival, we found a ride and a boat to the island. We had the chance to surf for two days. The waves were small enough to catch a few, but on the third day, I awoke the drums.... Oh no! Yep ... a real swell arrived, and I became a boat-bound cameraman ... it was huge.

So, the trip ended well ... we all had a good time and learned a lot about this type of wave. We decided to return during their summer (January) two years later. The same crew went with one addition ... Bret's friend BJ joined us. We arrived to a disappointed crew that was leaving the island ... they had been skunked ... all week, and no waves. We arrived as a summer swell filled in ... perfect size and shape.

We surfed for six days straight—had a blast. The food caused some illness ... nothing bad, but enough to be uncomfortable for a day or two. On Friday, Mel and I decided to try and get out on Saturday instead of Sunday, but the boys were also ready to go. We called the airlines, and (pre-9/11) there was no problem switching. In our group meeting, Bruce refused to leave a day early. Needless to say, it took us all by surprise.

The next day, everyone but Bruce piled into the boat and made the twenty-hour journey home. Bruce followed alone the next day. Yes, we abandoned him. I

104

felt bad but wanted to leave. Our decision left some hurt feelings for several years, but good surf healed the deal.

Sometimes, things happen for a reason. The trip taught me some valuable lessons. Years later, on some motorcycle runs with friends, we agreed to arrive separately, planning our trip in advance. So, no one had to do any hand-holding.

I still wish Bruce had gone with us or that we would have waited another day for him.

Look Out Below ...

It was 1959 ... it may have been 1960 ... but my memory of the experience could have been wrong. Danny and I went on a 'Juanita Holiday' to stay with Dad and Charlotte in NYC ... yep, NYC. And that freed Juanita to do whatever she did.

We were put on a Boeing 707 at LAX, and when we arrived in NYC, Jack was waiting. He lived in a flat off East 62nd and Second Ave. The building had 16 floors, and we were on the 8th. Being from Southern California, I had never been higher than our roof in Whittier, which I parachuted off by using a pillowcase. This was a whole new experience.

Jack and Charlotte had just brought Annie home, our newest sibling. I cannot even imagine how Charlotte ... the not-so-evil stepmother, could have handled this affair. Jack headed out to work each morning, and Char was left with an eleven- and nine-year-old, plus her first child, who could not have been more than a week or two old. Somehow, we all lived through it none the worse.

Danny and I went to play wiffle ball on the roof. I remember being freaked out when I looked over the side ... It might have been the "I'm going to jump for no

106

reason" syndrome. So, one day we were looking out the kitchen window, and the Safeway grocery union workers were picketing in front of the store. Danny walks over to the sink, fills a glass with water, and leans out the window. I squeezed in; he casually tipped the glass, and water dumped out like bombs from a plane; it was on course!

Danny stepped back quickly and closed the window. I looked at him, "What? Did we get them?"

"Don't open the window." I looked at him.

You would have to know Danny was a whack but very smart about these things. I, on the other hand, had no discipline. Yep, I had to know ... so I slid open the window, and we both peeked over the window ledge ... yep ... we got them. But, remember Danny said not to open the window? A cop looked up and saw us as he was counting floors.

We shut the window, "I told you so ... " he blurted out.

Charlotte was bathing Annie when the doorbell beckoned. Being a new mother, she was rattled yet confused about the situation.

"Who is it?" She asked. Danny and I knew.

The cop threatened juvenile hall if she didn't, "Keep us under tow." OK ... she was pissed.

107

At dinner, Charlotte told Jack what took place. We got the look of death, his famous scowl. After a brief pause in the dinner conversation, he said ... and this is a direct quote, "Did you get them?"

Charlotte was caught off guard ... Danny and I were confused ... and Jack was laughing ... he said, 'I hate the God Damn unions!' When the laughing died down, he took a serious moment to enlighten us of our punishment for a second offense. Did we learn ... nope ... we escalated to water balloons ... yep. I am not sure to this day, but if we had hit someone from the eighth floor, I think it would have seriously hurt them. That was not our intention ... indeed we had shifted targets ... we only did this once because the results actually rattled our tiny cages. I am certain Danny made the drop ... he was older and, therefore, a better shot. The next shot, a bright red balloon filled with water, about the size of a softball, hit dead center on the top of a NY cab. I actually saw it dent inwards. We closed the window immediately and watched TV for the rest of the afternoon—no doorbells ... no juvenile hall pissed-off Charlotte. Mission accomplished.

I wonder if the driver and his fare (if he had one) ever knew what hit them. Maybe he messed up his pants. The whole incident has me laughing right now as if it happened yesterday. We laughed our asses off. It was the last of our water balloon dropping; we calmed down and turned to paper airplanes.

On occasion, we actually made it through a door or windows.

We wrote on the wings, "Help ... I'm locked in the bathroom."

Bar Time

You have no idea what you can see and hear when you are in a bar 10 hours a day 6 days a week. Some of it is fun ... some of it is sad ... some of it is terrifying and then, at times, you are just confused. One night, I put a drink for a local on his tab while a stranger watched.

Afterward, I poured the new guy his drink. I asked for the cash, "Put it on my tab."

"You don't have a tab."

He looked at me and paid for his drink. It was getting busy when the stranger ordered another drink. I poured it and took his cash.

He says, "When you close the bar tonight, I'm gonna fuck you up."

I turned, "What?"

I weighed 98 lbs. dripping wet, and not a bar brawler. I was also smart enough to know that telling someone else would only cause the problem to worsen. The guy stayed all night and drank a lot. And every time I poured him a drink, he reminded me of his plan. As it got later, I started pouring him heavier and heavier drinks ... if he was gonna try and fuck me up, I thought if he was good and drunk, I might be able to escape. My actual state of mind was blank, but I was very concerned. As the night wound down, I announced the last call. He was still sitting at the end of the bar, wobbling but watching. I never said anything to anyone.

Finally, the locals left, and it was just us. "We have to exit the back door."

He nodded, got off his stool, and walked with me side by side out the back. He actually put his arm around my shoulders. My mental frame of mind is still foggy; however, I remember thinking my only chance was to make sure he never had kids. Believe me, I'd given it my best shot. Maybe I wasn't as afraid as I thought (yes, I was) maybe he was impressed with my silence and willingness to make that walk through the back door, maybe he thought I knew something (that I didn't) like Karate or Smith & Wesson.

Maybe he was a jerk or crazy because he started laughing out loud at 1 am in a country bar's deserted parking lot ... and he pushed me away and said, "I was only kidding ... I'm new around here ... can you give me a ride home?"

You fucker ... you unbelievable fucker ... and that was that ... I gave him a ride home. That was pretty much exactly how it happened. And you might agree with me that this was a weird deal ... but here's the weirder deal ... a few years later. I was going out for a beer with my neighbor and suggested this cheesy little bar instead of a pizza parlor. I wanted liquor, not beer. Our wives were on a road trip with the kids, and we were home hanging out and going to work. So, we went to this place called Gills. I was a heavy drinker at times, and that night was going to be one of those times. In the bar was a woman. Yes, a woman. One I should have stayed away from—a bartender I'd never seen, and I was getting drunker by the minute.

The bartender decided to buy me a drink. All I can say is I should have said no more. I blurted out, "I'm gonna fuck you up when you close tonight."

"What the fuck did you say?"

My friend practically spit his beer out, looked at me, and then the bartender. Then he stood up; he was 6'4" and weighed 240. Just hold on; it gets worse ... "I'm taking you home now." He threw me under his arm like a duck.

All I can say is thank you, God, for good (and large) friends. He threw me in the car and drove home. "Night out for a beer Uhhhh?"

FYI ... he never went for a drink with me again. Four years later, I got sober and made the world a safer place. He eventually asked me why I did that (we are, to this day, good friends). I replied, "I must have hit instant replay with a role reversal."

Early Salt Creek

If you surf or are from anywhere near Southern California, then you would know about Salt Creek. If you aren't familiar, then please let me fill you in.

In the early 1960s, it was one of those places off the map. You could actually drive down a dirt road and park right on the beach. Apparently (which means, as I remember it), these two old guys owned the road or the beach or both. They lived in this tiny house at the top of the road, and you had to check in with them to go down. My best guess is they charged for the experience. And the pot of gold at the end of the rainbow was a magnificent left-breaking wave off the point when conditions were good. So now you know.

Mark and I were in the summer between the 8th and 9th grade. I had a surfboard that I pulled behind my bike on a wooden rickshaw. Between drinking beers that Mark's brother bought and other juvenile activities, Mark made this thing we called a belly board. He cut the nose off of an old surfboard and resigned in a fin. He would lie on this thing and use surf fins to push himself into all sorts of waves. The apparatus was so cool I had to have one. So, I found a surfboard maker (Alexander) on Coast Highway who actually had one in his shop. Juanita always delivered and bought it the next day.

In '64, Newport Beach had just started licensing surfboards and limiting their use to certain locations during certain hours. It was a zoo and actually pretty dangerous. So, Mark convinced me to hitchhike to Salt Creek with our belly boards. We had been there a few times before with his brother, and apparently, it sounded like a good idea. Just like that, we are off. I do not remember anything about the ride we got, but back then, kids were always picking up other kids ... it was no big deal. Salt Creek is South of Laguna Beach ... just North of Dana Point. You would not recognize it today, thanks to the developers.

When we got to the top of the road, one of the old men who ran the place refused us entrance ... we were underage. What? That was not working, but he was adamant. Needless to say, his reluctance was not going to stop us. We did the only thing possible. Just north of the beach was a housing track, and we found a place to paddle out. It gave us access to the south point. After we headed out to hit the waves, the guy who refused us entrance saw us out on the water. He promptly tried to order us out of the water. Nah ... was not happening. We were feeling pretty good about our plan. The waves were big that day. Hang on while I explain what happened, as I remember. Some parts are unclear, but you will get the idea. Somehow, Mark lost his board ... we didn't have leashes back in the day. I still had my board, and when a wave came, I paddled over, and Mark would swim under. I never left him for long. As soon as he came up, we shared my board so he could catch his breath ... swimming under big waves as little tikes was a lot of effort.

As I recall ... after we had paddled quite a distance to the point and ridden a few waves, we were both tired. Not to mention, Mark was getting scared ... me too. After each set, I'd grab my board so we could rest. However, it did not take long before Mark was getting tired.

On our last wave, Mark said, "I'm too tired to do anymore."

"But you have to.... We came out here to surf. Come on, just go ..." To say I was scared is an understatement. If I lost the board, we did not have a chance. No matter; he dove under while I went over.

Once the wave passed, Mark flew out of the water, screaming, "I can touch, I can touch." He landed on a sandbar, which gave him time to rest.

Although we still needed to get the rest of the way, we were once again charged with that 14-year-old fearlessness. We obviously made it to shore that day and found a ride home. However, more of the story is foggy. I am sure we talked about everything. The old men on the beach never caught us but most likely yelled, demanding we not come back.

We went our separate ways at the end of that summer. But another time, probably circa 1987 ... I started bellyboarding again and called Mark. "I have two boards; do you still have some fins?"

He laughed, "Sure ... let's meet at 33rd Street in Newport Beach."

Our old favorite spot ... we rode some waves ... talked about life ... and sadly I haven't seen or spoken to him again. I am sure Salt Creek speaks to him once in a while, though. :)

First Burn

Monty, another pastime. One afternoon, I bought two-way radios and decided to take a trip. Monty took one radio, and I kept the other. We danced around the trucks, checked on stuff one more time, rolled up the I-5 Highway through central California, and headed east on I-80 to Reno. Upon our arrival, we checked into the hotel and went out to wander, eat, and gamble. In the morning, we had breakfast and stopped at the grocery store for our fresh fruit and some extra last-minute items ... Monty bought a condom! :)

Monty was ten years older than me and about the same number of years sober. Unfortunately, his wife had just passed away, so he was a bit lost. But when he learned of my plans to attend the Burning Man, he decided to come along. I brought this very cool painting wall that housed 9 framed canvases 4'x4' in size, plus all the paint required. The propane lanterns would light all night. Monty built an evaporation shower ... which was a hit. But best of all, he made over 500 glass necklaces that we gave away over the week. Together ... the painting wall and the necklaces made our camp popular.

When we arrived at our campsite, or address if you'd rather, we stepped out of our trucks and took a long look around. What an exciting time to be alive. And almost on queue, this flock of young women from next door came running over ... they were all topless. As the crowd explained, they were 'White Witches' from Victoria Island. At that time, neither one of us cared. They wanted to sprinkle us with violet moon water. Believe me, we took them up on the offer. Monty started passing out necklaces and helped put them on our ladies.

After camp was assembled, we looked around to find an amazing sight. People of all descriptions were working on projects, having the time of their lives. When we got back to camp, a very heavy wind came up and blew parts of the witch's camp down. At that exact moment, a soccer dad jumped out of his truck and helped us reassemble the girls' tents. Soon, everyone was OK again.

So, the guy ... Chuck was his name; had come alone and had no camp but wanted to hang out with us. The girls were so grateful they invited him to camp with them. What a blessing. Chuck changed immediately, and by the end of the week, he was wearing a tube top dress and staying out dancing all night. The neighborhood was a fun place, and just hanging around

119

after dark afforded me a great view of everything going on … including a 'disco golf cart' that rolled up at 2 am and shook the ground when it turned on … everyone came out and danced.

As I think about this entry, realizing that doing a quick overview of one's first Burning Man experience is impossible. So, I am going to pen it for a while. The girls next door were most entertaining. Every night, they would get dressed up (costumes are huge out there on the playa) and leave for a night on the town. One night, we were going to have a ceremony across the street, and one of the witches was going to lead. She took forever to get ready; the other girls were across the street with us. Finally, she emerged and crossed the street to join us … she was completely naked except for the knee-high boots she was wearing. Nudity at the "burn" is no big deal, so that did not affect anyone beyond a momentary pause to take in her nakedness. What flipped us all out simultaneously was what took her so long to get ready when all she put on was a pair of boots.

Then there was the "Man" … built in the center of the playa … sitting atop a structure that housed several viewing areas dedicated to representing most religions on the earth. The theme that year was "Beyond Belief," and it encouraged everyone to get beyond their chosen faith and take a humorous look back. On the playa was a phone booth that asked you to call God ... and when you picked up the receiver, a voice answered (sometimes male and sometimes female), "This is God ... how can I help you today?"

The center camp was a 24/7 activity ... three stages under a circus tent with no walls ... nonstop music, dancing, lectures, skits, and more music. And I do mean 24/7 nonstop. By Wednesday or Thursday, most things were built, and the city was alive and thriving ... it was nonstop throbbing ... mostly drums, rhythms, lights, and people lit up on bikes. Some were on foot, the playa cars that looked like giant submarines that played music, showed porn and shot off large propane cannons. It was a complete sensory overload.

I was there alone because that was how I rolled back then ... I was married with children ... one grown and one nearly grown ... but I had been doing the adult things alone forever. And then one night, at the witch's camp, one of them asked if she could camp with me because I didn't venture out much that year ... at least not to dance and drink, and never for very long. So, we had a great evening together and spent the next two days as one. We talked about ourselves nonstop, listening to each other. Oblivious to everything and everyone else. On the last day, we said our goodbyes.

Not without emotions, not without fear, but also a long, slow goodbye that burned us deeply. "Hey, will you promise to be with me in my next life?" She asked.

"Yes, of course," I replied.

On the way home, Monty and I talked at a restaurant late at night just before the final highway push. I was confused and a little dazed because I had crossed a line, not the physical one, and not a defined one that was tied to dishonesty. However, it was not innocent either. It was just an experience that would be hard to shake. Monty was so cool; he just said ... remember ... she was the messenger, not the gift. You deserve someone like her, but not her.

Besides a million other things that happened that week, we had some memorable moments to never forget. The first "burn" is almost impossible to describe. It is like taking a picture of the Grand Canyon and then looking at it when you get home. Where did the grandiosity go? Where was the indescribable escape? Perhaps back into one's soul, hey!

Monte moved to another dimension a few years later while I progressed in the spirit. He is missed. However, it's not fair to hang the outcomes on Burning

Man, although very few can say they did not leave as a better person.

8

Jane's Donkey

Do you remember Fred and Jane, who owned that little ranch? The one that I taught to throw boulders at Fred's Cadillac when he drank and would not unlock the door? Or, at least, threaten to throw boulders. Actually, I loved that little rented house in the back of the ranch. Nevertheless, thinking back, I am not sure why I moved.

After moving, I stopped in regularly to ride their little horse called "Wahaka." He was a pistol, but he loved me. Most everyone else just left him alone, but man, he was fast. In fact, most of the time, he spent on his hind legs.

I am wondering just a touch because they were very close friends. Some of my fondest memories involve them. Anyway, here is just one funny story.

One morning, I decided to sleep in, and Jane called, in a frantic voice, "Fred is not home … can you come over right away? Our donkey needs help.

"Yes, I'll be right there."

I grabbed some clothes, jumped in my car, and headed over. When I arrived, she was waiting out front. "Come quick, our donkey had a baby." She was frantic.

"Wait ... What?"

"She had a baby and won't let it nurse."

"Uhhhh ..." I did not know what to say. Apparently, if foals don't nurse right away, they might die. Who knew? Not me! "Okay, what do you want me to do?"

"I need help tying the mother to the fence so the baby can drink."

I stared at her for a moment, "Are you serious about tying up the mother?"

"Yes. She weighs more than both of us together."

"We have to try; I don't know what else to do."

Well, the donkey wanted nothing to do with our plan. She reared up at us and stomped her feet. We jumped quickly to avoid her hooves. I tried everything I could think of to calm her down, but nothing worked. "I think you better call the vet. One of us is going to get hurt."

At the time, I must have been 22, and Janie maybe 25. Fred happened to be older but was MIA. She kept his whereabouts quiet, and I did not ask. Jane called the vet, who came immediately. We discussed the problem quickly, and she grabbed a needle. Relax, it's not what you might be thinking; it was a tranquilizer just to calm the mother. I am sure the mother was scared; she had just given birth and was unsure of the process. Jane may have freaked her out before she could get her balance ... who knows. But once the tranquilizer took hold, she calmed, and the foal walked over and started nursing. The drama was over.

As I recall, Fred showed up after everything settled, so I left. Other than that, the day was a mystery. Maybe I went to the checkdams and got drunk or downtown to the laundry mat or to the cafe for breakfast or the bar for a beer. It was just another day.

Dirt Merchant, Hippie, Marine, and Cowboy Bar

At 23, I was a bartender that lasted one year. The new owner hired me to gain local business. It worked pretty well. In this case, it was to hire a young local, and the youngsters would come. And come they did ... spending money, having fun, and bringing their friends. Once he added music on the weekends, the other locals loved it as well. The 'flatlanders' (people from downtown) came too. So, as you can see, we had a wild group that sometimes mixed well and other times didn't play so well together.

One Marine that always drank Coors beer and, for the most part, was quiet ... and at the same time likable and worthy of your respect. I was always in the middle of some controversy. Bartenders often are, but he always calmed me when trouble kicked up. I'd see him motioning to get him another beer.

Then he said, "Relax, it's nothing to worry about, I got your back."
In most cases, nothing happened, but it was comforting to have him around. However, one night, a hippie and he got drunk, and for some reason, the hippie got violent

with the Marine. After considerable effort to talk the hippie out of his mood, the Marine finally picked him up and drove him to the ground through a table and chairs.

"You're not worth the trouble." He replied.

Oblivious of how lucky the hippie's first encounter was, he attacked him again. The Marine repeated the first knockdown. Only, this time, he left the bar and went home.

Only the story does not end on this note. The hippie knew where the Marine lived. In a small town, you know everyone. After pulling up out front, the hippie stood outside yelling at him.

The Marine yelled, "Don't come in; I will shoot you."

As time passed, the hippie got more pissed. But knew what the end result would be if he pushed any further. So, instead, he hopped in his truck, peeled out in reverse, and backed into a ditch. After trying to get out, he couldn't, so he asked for help. The Marines did help. He put his gun in the drawer and walked out to help.

Another guy we called 'nipple nuzzler' because he was always bumping against women, and they never seemed to mind. He was a nice guy, and the ladies loved him. But there was this canyon backlash towards the people from downtown as though they didn't belong in the canyon. This was completely crazy ... we needed their money!

One night, he got pretty drunk, and remember, he was a nice guy, not a tough case, but that didn't matter this time. He turned to the guy sitting next to him ... a complete stranger ... and just knocked him right off his bar stool with one punch. The 'nuzzler' was a pretty big guy. He got up and called the guy on the floor a 'flatlander' then walked out. Not one person said a thing to him or even considered asking what that was all about. Another guy helped the stranger back up onto his barstool.

Now, remember, bartenders know everything...he asked me why he treated a total stranger like that.... My only answer was to hand him a free drink and move on.

Then there was this really big guy who played bass in a local rock band and drank expensive Scotch in larger bucket glasses until he would literally pass out. Then, it took at least three guys to hustle him across the road to his house, where his wife always said to put him on the couch.

One night, there was a young guy who had just been released from prison and was not supposed to be in a bar, but there he was, drinking, two-fisted. He and the bass player had some sort of conversational collision, and the young guy got hot.

The bass player ignored the incident and left his barstool. He leaned back on his chair against the wall and complied with the 'never turn your back in a bar' rule. The young guy implied he had a weapon. I did not know if he did or not. He sat down and began to tell me ... remember ... the bartender not only knows everything but must also listen to everything—he said he was going to take the big guy out before the night is done. I really didn't need the trouble and liked the bass player. When he came back for another drink, I leaned over and warned him.

"Hey," he smiled. "The only thing I like more than fucking, is fighting." He proceeded to drink himself unconscious.

In any case, he was too big and scary to worry about some skinny young kid. The night ended peacefully.

My last night on the job was my birthday. I really behaved myself and did not even drink. Usually, I drank in sync with the crowd ... the heavier they drank, the heavier I drank. It worked out. Late that night, two girls I knew 'well' came in and wanted to buy me a birthday drink. I refused.

They insisted, "Alright, I will make a Soft Shoe. We can share it." It was the early version of a Long Island Iced Tea.

We all put a straw in the glass and counted 1 ... 2 ... 3, and then we drank the entire bucket in about 5 seconds. It was good ... loosened us up and I immediately made another and another and finally got lost. I loved those girls ... they were the best. I did remember to put the booze away at 2 am (California law), but I never closed the joint, and a lot of people were there and having a great time, so we pumped coins into the jukebox and partied on. Eventually, the owner came flying in, yelling and screaming and threw everybody out ... including me. I remember it was 3:30 am. I saw him grab the cash out of the drawer (oops ... I forgot to do the bank) in anger, and bills flew everywhere. I'm not sure about feeling guilty for letting him down, but it was my official last day on the job. I was getting married that weekend and I even knew you just can't close a bar at 2 am and expect to stay married for long. :)

My Gun

It so happens my brain is fogging on how the gun came into my possession, but it was not stolen. I believe it came from a friend. Times were different, and although I was not and am still not now a gun enthusiast, I know getting them was easy.

The gun was a .22 caliber built on a Colt 45 frame. It was a single-action six-shooter. It came with a tan leather holster and belt that held bullets. I got it when I was living on Fred and Janie's ranch.

My early bird-killing days were behind me, so I set bottles up in my small pasture. I used to shoot for quite a while at a time. It was a small caliber handgun that was made to look like a Colt 45 replica but had a longer barrel than most, therefore somewhat reliable. Like the BB gun from years earlier, I learned how to compensate for its flaws.

Although target practice was fun, I needed more (there's a shocker), so I moved into the quick draw. I was getting better until I somehow discharged the gun, pulling it out of the holster ... it fired into the ground right next to my foot. I put the gun down, and that was the end of my "Billy the Kid" era ... time to move on again.

The next phase was my "fan the hammer," and I rolled off all six rounds in rapid succession. The ammo went a little quicker, but it was fun for a while. Finally, the novelty of walking out the backdoor and shooting faded. So, my gun fetish waned until one sunny morning when Fred, Janie, and another girlfriend saddled up three horses and rode out the back gate.

In a couple of minutes, Fred came galloping back through the gate. "What's up," I hollered.

"A rattler," he yelled.

"Gotta get my rifle."

I grabbed my pistol and ran with Fred, sighting the snake. We rounded the first bend, and the two girls were sitting on their horses in the middle of the road, watching this magnificent red diamondback rattler coiled and rattling away.

We stopped a few yards from the snake; I stood behind Fred with my gun loaded and in hand. Fred drew a bead with his .22 cal. Long rifle. As he squeezed off a round, some dust billowed in front of the snake.

Before Fred prepared his second round, I slid to the right of his hip and fanned off all six rounds in seconds. Then, there was silence except for the ringing in my ears. I remember seeing the snake bounce around a bit and dust flying everywhere.

Fred was pissed, not because I killed the snake. But because I used plastic-headed bullets that act like a mini shotgun. It ruined Fred's perfect hat band idea. He wanted a headshot to spare the skin. Fred was a great guy and, by now, a good friend, so he wasn't really mad, just astonished that I shot six rounds in seconds. Not to mention my accuracy. He skinned the snake anyway and made his hatband, even with the holes. :)

A couple of years later, after leaving the ranch, I rented a place across the street from a small bar. The house had a set of dark steps partially hidden by ivy, leading up the canyon wall. Of course, I spent many nights at the bar. So, trouble broke out many evenings. Biker clubs used to hang out, which included many weapons for sure.

My roommate was a heavy drinker, an ex-Marine who was missing a front tooth from his early hockey days on the East Coast. Nevertheless, he had a bad habit of slapping people a little too hard on the back when he'd walk up to them.

One night in the parking lot, he slapped the wrong guy ... a very dangerous local dirt merchant. In seconds, the guy knocked him down with a vicious blow and jumped on him. Nobody could stop the fight and a few guys were even encouraging it to continue. Jeff was getting killed, but being a bull himself, it might have turned bad.

The fight kept raging, and someone had to stop the battle. So, I ran up across the street, through the ivy, loaded my gun, and came back ready to stop the fight. Although, I had a moment of clarity when I hit the bottom of the steps. Jeff would probably live, the dirt merchant would probably die, and I'd definitely spend the rest of my life in jail. I tossed the gun in the ivy and gathered another friend to save Jeff and stop the fight. At that exact moment, another kid walked out the back door, broke a beer bottle, and stuck the jagged edge in the dirt merchant's head. He let Jeff go, so we snatched him up, scared off a few of his friends, and dragged him home.

I retrieved the gun the next day, cleaned it up, and eventually sold it for $25. The guy who bought it gave it back when it misfired. I wrapped it in rags, stuck it in a zipper bag, and 39 years later, it's still in my ex-wife's garage—she doesn't know. :)

Today, my house is gun-free, except for a brief moment. It's wrapped up with the other one, too! A friend's mother was some sort of 'past life reader.' I enjoyed her psychic readings. She would lean her head back, close her eyes, and start telling me of events in my past life. She said it was like her watching a movie! One of her readings included guns. I happened to have died from a gunshot during the Civil War. Whether you believe that stuff or not ... whether it is true or not ... guns have always made me nervous, and I will never hold one again ... lest I shoot something!

Uncle Joe's Shot Gun

So, while we are on the topic of guns...another episode comes to mind. My friend Mark and his older brother, Rex, and I were good friends. He would buy us beer during the summer. And we stored our surf gear at his house. It never failed though. Rex was always in the wrong place at the wrong time. As brothers, they were very close.

Mark and I spent a lot of time shooting birds with my .22 cal pump pellet gun. Although there was no gunpowder, it was every bit as lethal. I remember the carnage we caused with that gun and regretted it deeply over the years. In fact, I am sure some of my 'bad luck' was actually just 'bad karma' from those kills. I may never be done with that debt in this lifetime ... and I have no idea why guns and birds were so much a part of my life.

One day, Mark invited me to go shooting in the desert. His father was taking Rex's motorcycle to him somewhere in or near Death Valley. Mark had access to a 12-gage shotgun. I believe it was an over-under, not a side-by-side double-barrel version. My Uncle Joe had a side-by-side double barrel 20-gauge shotgun. I borrowed it, and off to the desert we went with a ton of ammo. We were fourteen at the time.

When we got there, Mark's father just turned us loose on the desert valley ... maybe that is where Rex got his craziness from ... lack of parenting from the start. We were on the hunt for birds. But there were no birds in the desert ... at least none that we could find! So, every now and then, we would see a lizard make a dash across a clearing and 'blam blam.' Or unload; you don't really find the kill when it's 5 or 6 inches long and gets hit by two rounds of shotgun pellets. We were fast and usually shot many rounds at anything that moved.

As the day wore on, we got increasingly anxious to find something of substance to shoot. Again, I cannot recall understanding why this was important. I guess living in Pocatello as a young boy and going hunting with the men could have influenced me, but they were in the habit of eating what they killed ... not us. We saw a pond in the distance and were on the move. As we approached, swimming in the pond was a duck. It was like a race ... we leveled our guns and triggered them at the same moment. It really sounded like a single shot, but both guns kicked and smoked.

There was a moment where everything stood still ... we watched as the gush of water rose into the air and fell back to the surface, but the duck was gone. We buried it with two loads of buckshot. Then, we noticed the small shed or house to the side of the pond. Remember, we didn't approach or case the situation. We came upon the pond, the duck, and we fired immediately. Only after that moment did we bother to look around. The sight horrified us ... we started running and didn't stop for quite a while. What if it had been a pet duck or something like that?

We ran into Rex, who had been looking for us. He had a semi-automatic .22 cal rifle. When we got close, maybe fifty or hundred feet, he started firing over our heads and laughing at us. We were terrified. The bullets whizzed over our heads, and not just one or two but several. Mark began screaming at Rex to stop ... I just watched ... frozen in horror.

But Rex was laughing and firing intermittently, but Mark leveled his 12 gauge and yelled, "Stop, or I'll shoot," He hollered. "I swear to God, Rex."

Rex stopped and came over laughing. Mark and I did find it funny. Later that afternoon, we piled in the car with Mark's Dad and headed home. We were rolling down a deserted highway when we noticed a bunch of crows resting on the telephone wires. As we drove past, we begged Mark's dad to stop and let us take a shot ...

he refused ... reminding us that we would probably miss or damage the electric wires. On the way home, we laughed remembering the duck ... laughing as we did. I never shot Uncle Joe's shotgun again.

Drunken Artists

Part of this story holds sections that cause me guilt to this day. I acknowledge the sadder side of my life. It's pretty revealing to write certain instances in one's past. Especially when your actions are less than admirable. Now, I see them as incomprehensible demoralization. But remember, during the experience, it was fun.

At the time, we lived in Laguna Beach and it was close to the Summer Sawdust Festival. A friend came over, and we decided to hang out one night. He owned a bike, but not me. So, we chose to steal one. We'd been drinking and smoking all day, and that meant stealing a bike sounded easy. He drove me up and down a few streets until I saw a bike lying near the curb. I hopped out ... grabbed it, and rode away.

At that moment, the guilt set in, but I was already moving and just stuffed those feelings away. I flipped the 'have fun' switch.

At any rate, stoned and ready for fun, we headed for the festival. We brought some wine along to enhance our high. When we got there ... this was spontaneous... I am sure it was Brent's thought, as well. We sat down in an unmanned booth with a sign on the fence that simply said pay at the gate if you want to buy something. There were several paintings hanging on the walls and two folding chairs. We settled in and kept drinking and essentially became 'the artists.' In a few minutes some people stopped and were looking at the paintings.

"Are you one of the artists?" They asked.

"Yes, I am," Brent replied.

They had a great conversation about Brent's feelings while he painted the piece. He was very convincing. Needless to say, they bought the painting.

The artist got the money ... we had the fun. Suddenly, we were on a roll for the next couple of hours. We drank, met people, and pretended to be artists. I have no recollection of sales or anything clear, as we were drunk, stoned, and killing memory cells. I do remember it was really fun, along with the flowing bullshit. Luckily, the real artist never returned, but after the wine was finished, we folded the chairs, cleaned up, and left. It was our little secret.

After we got back, some friends and everyone decided to hit the Round Table bar down on Main Street. But karma smacked me. My stolen bike had been stolen ... go figure ... goes around ... comes around. So, we went back to the house and grabbed my VW. I am not sure why ... but we drove down the hill to the bar. I was only twenty, but someone handed me a fake ID ... it was a done deal. I'm in. About the only thing I really remember was being wasted. The bartender took one look at me, "You need to leave."

"Fuck you ..." I short-circuited.

"I fought in Vietnam for your fucking freedom; now pour me a drink." He said, "If you do not leave, I will call the police."

"Did you not hear me? I fought for this country, and you can't stop me from buying a drink." Needless to say, he called the police.

"Hey, dude. You better leave." Brent shouted.

I stumbled out the door and ran right into two city police officers. It was not good being drunk, angry, and underage. Of course, when they asked for ID, I gave them the fake ID. It gets worse in my state of mind. I had not looked at the ID. So, when they asked my name and age, nothing matched. Apparently, I was much older and lived in Oakland, CA!

Brent followed me out, offering to drive me home. Apparently, I drank much heavier than the others because the police were actually okay with that idea. But before Brent could not get me moving to the car. My drunken stupor caused me to reach up and flip one of the policeman's helmets. It rolled off the back of his head and into the gutter that was filled with water.

He snapped, "That's it … you are going to jail." They slapped on the cuffs, picked me up by my collar and belt, and slid me in the back seat of the squad car. To say the least, it was a nightmare. When I look back on these instances, nothing seems real. I was out of control, yelling insults and fighting to get free.

I screamed, "I am not a pot-smoking hippie (with my hair in a ponytail). I have a job, and you suck."

Before long, the other inmates were yelling at me to shut up. But, instead of listening, I just threatened to kick their asses. Yep … I had flown over the cuckoo's nest that night for sure.

A few hours later, a really nice policeman, I mean a really nice policeman, woke me up slowly.

"Look, if you really have a job, I will book you quickly and let you go. But you have to behave. Can you do that?"

"Yes," I replied.

So, needless to say, I cooperated and was out in thirty minutes. I actually had a job at the stained-glass shop in the canyon. My shift started at 7 am. The court stuff got settled, and I paid off the fine.

It's still amazing that I never blacked out that night. The incident was painful; it started with stealing a bike and ended with a cop being very kind and caring about me. Back then, nothing really impressed me. But, tonight, thinking about what happened and my actions, it's a wonder the cop was nice. Maybe he had a son just my age.

9

Bluffing

After completing a 12-hour shift on the paper folding machine at work, I headed home in my '57 VW. The radio worked, thank goodness; however, it only ran on two cylinders. Earlier that day, I had scored some pot and decided to smoke some on my way home. I worked from 2 pm to 4 am. I finished a job and would be a hero for doing it before I left. Since my house was in the foothills, at four in the morning, it was unusual to see any other cars on the road.

At some point, my half-smoked joint ended up on the floor of my car. It wasn't going to burn anything important, but needless to say, I needed to put it out. So, I pulled over, and while kneeling outside the car rummaging through the floorboard, searching for the doobie, a sheriff's car pulled up behind me. Since my attention remained on finding the joint and the radio blaring, I didn't hear anything until someone cleared their throat.

I picked up my head, seeing the flashing lights through my armpit dam. "So, what are you doing?"

"I have engine trouble."

He looked at me in disbelief, "In the front seat of a VW?"

Once he had me leaning against his car, he went to inspect mine. Of course, he came back with the two bags of pot I had bought on my lunch break. I looked at him with literally no defense.

I had never sold anything; I was a user, not a dealer. But since there were two bags in the car, he could arrest me for possession, intent to sell, and transportation of narcotics. It was 1972. I worked sixty hours a week, had long hair, and, other than just being stupid, I was a pretty cool guy. In reaction and to save my ass, I said, "You know when you get home tonight and pour a Martini, you are going to think of me in jail for 10 years for working hard and smoking pot. Am I doing anything different than you?" "There is no one around, and I'm not bothering anyone." Yes, I was driving with illegal pot, but he got my drift.

My initial response was to no avail because we headed downtown. However, by the time we got to the station, he had changed his mind.

"Why did you have two bags?"

"I buy two at a time, so I don't have to make this trip twice as often."

He turned to the desk Sergeant, "Book him on a misdemeanor possession charge."

Fortunately, I got lucky again. It could have gone the other way easily, and my life would have ended a lot differently. I received my phone call, and I called my brother Dan.

"Hey, bro, can you go get my paycheck and then at 7 am go to the bail bonds office and get me outta here?" Dan said he would do that and hung up

The whole incident happened early Friday morning and when I was having lunch that day, I began to realize Dan had not arrived yet. I spent the next three days in the 72-hour holding tank. The worst of the worst were held there waiting for their court appearance. I could fill another book with the experiences I went through, but I won't. It will suffice to say that it is possible to get jailed for a small offense and then spend the rest of your life in prison for what happened in the holding tank.

My roommate realized that when my dog came home without me, something had happened. He made one call and immediately headed to the bail office and got me out.

Once they let me out, I called my brother. "I am so sorry ... I went back to sleep and forgot." Really, I forgot for three days!

This story pertains to bluffing because it explains why the DMV called me in for a hearing. After all, I had been driving under the influence! After I got to the meeting, we went into this room with four to five old men my dad's age.

They were all deciding whether to suspend my license. Hindsight, they should have. "Go ahead; I'll live on unemployment and spend my days on the beach, enjoying life while your taxes support me and buy groceries with my food stamps."

Now, what I really wanted to say was, "Please don't do that ... I won't be able to get to work without a car, and without a job, I will soon be living under a bridge."

The men were genuinely surprised with my answer ... there was even silence in the room. Finally, one of them took the initiative and answered my brashness.

"We are going to issue a warning on your license, and the next time, we will take it away."

In that day and age, with no insurance, the penalty had as much effect as hitting me with a feather pillow.

"Ok," I said, "Can I go now?"

The Voice of God in the Wrong Train

The title of this story is very intriguing, but I need to give you some context beforehand. I spent much of my time in London trying to become a great musician. But let's get real for a moment. It's been over thirty years since I started playing the guitar and keyboard. Actually, I've played all of the instruments except the drums. Not to mention, I found a semi-soul mate who learned the melodies from my weak renditions and poured her heart into making them come to life. But, as stated, let's get real for a moment. I ain't no musician. In fact, when I was a boy in church, I was asked to listen and not sing along. Yep ... I am that bad.

In another story, I wrote about a miraculous escape I was a part of after a disastrous gig at a London high school. So even with a supporting cast, I sucked big time. But that never kept me from pushing forward.

In my early days, I hooked up with a British kid who had a plan to go down in history as the 'Old Man of Pop.' No joking aside, he could have accomplished the task. In fact, he almost did in 1969. Along with another guitarist and me, he called his band "Chaplin." But here's the deal—I was not capable of pulling off the musical side of the arrangement. Sebbie, the songwriter was, and said, "No worries, we'll skip you on guitar. You are an actor, as am I, and I need your stage presence with me."

Apparently, he liked the image we were going to project. Since hiring a guitarist was easy, and no one would know, we had our course set.

The guy could write, his lyrics were off the chart, so was his 'aura.' An incredibly creative mind. Once, I even embedded a paragraph from one of his songs in an essay for a high school senior English assignment.

I had one foot in an American curriculum high school and one in London. One foot nearly in the Rock N' Roll Hall of Fame. And let's not forget my lack of musical talent, nor could I carry a tune. The day after I turned my paper in, the teacher asked me to stay after class ... oh boy!

She asked, "You added the paragraph in quotation marks, but it's not your writing?"

"No, it is not mine," I replied.

"Do you know who wrote this?"

"Yes."

"He is a genius. This is the most well-written and controlled piece of writing I have ever read. Can I meet your friend?"

"No, that's not going to happen." Mysterious was numero uno on the writer's agenda!

That night, I stepped onto a London Underground train with an old, shabby acoustic guitar. I had stepped into an underground rail car that was full of drunken English football fans. Back in the 60s, it was a regular event for these crowds to trash entire trains in a drunken brawl. As soon as the doors closed, I was trapped in hippie clothing and long hair, carrying that old guitar. Boy, did the insults start when the drunks were demanding that I play them a song. Now remember ... I'm not a musician. I am an actor!

The scene got hostile. I gripped the guitar's neck, thinking I'd hurt at least one of them before they beat me like a drum. It was an awkward moment. I was not and am not a big guy. But I was in their world, in the wrong clothes, and at the wrong time ... oops! And then, right out of heaven, comes the voice of God from this burly, ruff-looking man who had been sitting quietly across the aisle from me. He says in a monotone, don't fuck with my voice, "Leave the lad alone; he's done nothing to you."

None of the drunk rowdies said a word. They backed away, and the train stopped, and I backed off, keeping an eye on everyone and nodding at my savior. Like I said ... I ain't no musician.

Falling Mentor

My life needed organization. Here I was, nearly twenty-four, about to get married, and did nothing but skip from one gig to the next. The printing business was steady work and suited my personality well; however, my impulsivity got me to quit and take up a bartending job. It lasted almost a year and ended with nothing to show for the experience.

The last day I was at work in the print shop before becoming a bartender, the small press I ran stopped working properly at the same time the repair guy walked out.

While attempting to fix the machine, my boss walked by, "Why is this machine not running?"

Drama Queen response, "I am going to have a nervous breakdown if this does not get fixed."

My boss remained skeptical. "Why don't you take a week off? If you still want the job, I will hold it for you. But you need to think it over."

It was just the response that I wanted to hear. It gave me the perfect excuse. I dropped the hammer I was getting ready to beat that press with, punched out, and went home. As I pulled into the canyon, the local bar was open across the street. Oh, what the hell ... I walked in, sat down, and ordered a beer.

The owner walked over, "Hey, why don't you hire me?" I asked.

He looked over and smiled. So, it gave me a week off, and I started as a bartender the following week.

For the next year, I had a good time working behind the bar. I learned a lot and got a little older and wiser. I was nearing the end of this job as I was going to get married in a few weeks. Closing at 2 am and working every weekend in a bar would not work in a marriage. So, option A came back into play. However, the economy was bad, and work was slow and limited. I went back to the shop I had left and saw that they were really slow and needed work. I told the Forman I could find them work. He took me to the owner, who took me to lunch and hired me on the spot to start in sales. Don, the company owner, came into my life. In three years, I got two cars. Sales did not come easy, but with proper training, I excelled.

My success went so well that I left that company and started my own business. Needless to say, Don was furious. He threatened to follow me around and give my clients free printing to drive me out of business. I never actually intended to steal his clients.

My relationship with my new partner and shop did more than just survive the next six years. It flourished in all areas, including money. In the end, a savant partner bought my share, and I promised to stay away from his clients.

It was nice to receive something for the clients I brought into the company. However, if you look at the business deal now, it seems tiny. The sale got me seventeen thousand and a Ford truck and camper. After that, Don welcomed me back with open arms to my sales position.

Only the perks did not stop; he bought me a brand-new Porsche and gave me a credit card for business expenses. Don's lifestyle with alcohol and drugs was literally killing me. I stayed for three years, went to rehab, and got sober. Unfortunately, Don did not. The money, yes, was good, but it was not easy to watch Don throw his life away. Eventually, another opportunity dropped in my lap. But Don was not pleased with my success and resented me. It was time to give back the credit card and car and leave. So, needless to say, we parted on bad terms. A good decision on my part.

The choice quickly proved fruitful; my career launched to a place unimaginable. But, through the grapevine, I heard Don lost his loan and all four plants.

It really hit me hard; my first mentor fell apart. While in rehab, Don paid me my base salary. It was hard because, no matter what I needed, he was always there for me. Once my rehab ended, I searched him out and asked if he would have lunch with me.

At first, he said, "No. I don't want to talk about anything that happened."

The news hit me hard, "But Don, you are the reason for my success. Everything I have is because of you. You pulled me out of the gutter; you believed in me. My own father refused to co-sign on the car loan. But you bought me a new Porsche." He accepted.

We met at the most expensive restaurant I could find, and we had a great lunch. I kept my promise and never brought up his business. The conversation is a mystery, but we were able to mend fences. It was the last time I saw him; hard to believe it was twenty-three years ago. We never saw each other again.

In closing, he was not an idol but a mentor and friend ... and I choose to remember him that way. He probably didn't get that part of the equation ... but I will never forget it.

Don't Come by Every Day

Over the years, I have come to believe what goes around comes around, and we deserve everything that happens to us. However, that does not mean we always understand the reason behind the experiences.

I have talked a little about my childhood ... or lack of it ... but sometimes I want to sit and cry. I have no idea how Danny deals with it ... or Annie, Julie, or John. Still, I know we all deal with similar issues. Basically, Jack was unavailable for us most of the time. Life with Juanita was a project ... and Charlotte was very quiet.

I ruined my life long before London ... but found ways to move further from this planet. In 1967, Juanita was diagnosed with breast cancer. My life, by that time, had moved so far down the line that the only person who mattered was me. The rest of my family stepped up to take care of my mom. At the time, I really had no understanding of the situation.

In the hospital, before surgery, Juanita said, "Don't let Tommy get into any more trouble."

"What is she talking about?" my aunts asked.

I shrugged. Juanita recovered, she came home and the party continued. At the time, after my childhood experience, she was the last person I wanted to be around. The only thing that mattered was me. The success of my career and money continued to get me into more trouble.

Eventually, I called Jack. "Please help."

"Yes, what do you need?"

He tried to help in his own way, but it was to no avail. I was too far gone. Jack had a gruff exterior, but inside, he cared deeply. In fact, at the funeral, Jack sat next to me for support. Juanita died ten years later. It was easy since I felt nothing.

London happened to be my downfall ... It only drove me deeper into the death spiral. It's amazing that I finished high school. Jack went to graduation, but my problems did not allow me to get my diploma—then, it was mailed. I remember not wanting to stay and the police demanding me to wait until after the event.

But underneath it all, I was still a small child looking for something to believe in. I had a job ... made $3.00 an hour, and rode an old Honda 305 Scrambler motorbike to get around. Jack and Charlotte brought their kids and Nanny to Southern California for home leave that summer. The idea of having other kids around was exciting. Juanita had moved to Hawaii between her first and second surgery. By then, I was living in the foothill canyon with a few friends. So, I couldn't wait to see everyone. Only when they arrived did it prove what a bad son I had been and the chaos I had created. Jack, at that time, was beyond forgiveness. However, it went way beyond the trouble. I spent much of life wondering about it, trying to figure out how I fit into the universe. My first visit to their rented beach house is non-existent in my memory. I had ridden the only wheels I had, my Honda Motorbike, to see everyone. Jack pulled me aside before I left.

He said, "It's ok to stop by once in a while, but don't come every day."

The words cut deep. I was shattered. I started the bike and looked at him with complete disdain while literally dying inside. The open road gave me freedom; my bike hit 90 mph. All I remember was hoping something serious would happen ... a flat ... a seized engine, or something. My insides were ripped apart, I was so fucking lonely. Just utterly sad; nothing mattered.

Well, of course, nothing happened, hence penning this book. I hit the next beach and downshifted back to reality. We made our beds ... I closed my heart, wiped the tears, and never looked back.

Years later ... after a final rupture ... we were friends and actually developed a love for each other at a distance. I tried to find a connection, but we never bonded over anything. When Jack became terminal, the news hit me. It wasn't supposed to happen, but he succumbed and died. The last thing I remember was him squeezing my hand ... he was so weak ... and no voice left, so he mouthed the words ... I love you, Tommy.

Daily Incantation

Our Father in Heaven

(this would be where each of our Gods or spiritual connections to a better way of living appears)

Hallowed be thy name.

(based on the existence of this other elevated level of consciousness, we must admit it rocks)

Your Kingdom Come

(this assumes that everyone at the same time understands the same thing)

Thy Will be done

(here is where it gets tricky ... the concept becomes a reality when "right" actions flow through all of us)

on Earth as it is in Heaven

(here, we get a visual of this higher level of consciousness existing in its perfect form ... somewhere else)

Give us this day our daily bread.

(this has to be spiritual nourishment ... it cannot mean food ... who eats in heaven?)

Forgive us of our debts

(again ... this would have to mean the absolution of our human traits ... not a bank loan, hey)

as we forgive our debtors

(and now, to make it all work ... we, in turn, forgive everyone who has committed humanity on us)

and lead us not into temptation

(hold that thought ... do not think you can have your cake and eat it too)

but deliver us from evil

(and now we confront the dark side of a higher consciousness that would have us eat the cake)

for thine is the Kingdom and Power and Glory forever.

(this is optional flattery that should be taken in context ... if we achieve the former, we have the latter)

God grant us the serenity to accept the things we cannot change

(here we get into reality ... progress not perfection ... is better than damnation)

the courage to change the things we can

(this would not be people, places, or things ... this would be the thoughts in our heads being bad)

and the wisdom to know the difference

(do not beat your head against a wall ... if you run into one ... either turn left or right ... but keep moving)

we pray only for your will for us today

(we are hoping we can keep centered long enough to make it through the day without blowing it up)

and the courage to carry it out

(rubber meeting the road comes to mind ... either we do or we don't ... there is no "trying")

every day, we are getting better and better and better

(practice makes nearly perfect nearly all of the time)

our improvement is for the improvement of all mankind

(getting better is a way of saying we are letting go of the darker side ... that can help everyone you know)

we are in complete control of our faculties ...

(we are not whack)

and our sensing devices ...

(meaning we can read others' feelings)

and our outer sensing devices

(this would include a connection to a side that is intuitive in all us ... free from our control)

positive images will bring to us things that we desire.

(anything is possible ... just ask the Wright Brothers)

In closing ... I am not being flip ... it is just that for years ... as I struggled to escape my demons and sadness ... I would say these prayers like a mantra ... repeatedly until they just became words ... I did this often while I was running miles and miles and miles. There is some connection there, for sure. And one day, as I was running along, oblivious to the pain, the words began to resonate. I hope you enjoyed ... agnostics or atheists as well. :)

10

I Can't ... It's My Brothers' Friends Boss's Pickup

As the stories of my life unfold in these pages, many are out of chronological order. So, if you find they jump from place to place in time or even time zones, it is because much of my life is a blur. But the memories are all real ... the times have changed because I can't remember shit.

The next story takes place between living in the canyon and selling everything to sail on a purse-saner tuna boat to the Ivory Coast of Africa. However, I actually missed the boat, so I ended up moving in with my brother Danny.

Danny and some of his friends were sitting around getting stoned, so I asked to borrow a vehicle and drive up to the canyon and visit some friends.

Danny's friend says, "Sure ... take the pickup, but get it back tonight, or I'm in big trouble ... it's my boss's truck."

I finished another beer, took a hit or two off the weed, and wandered out to the canyon. The actual destination is unknown, but to my best recollection, it was to Chuck's house. He lived with his girlfriend but had a sister with whom I had slept before. In fact, I was hoping to climb into bed with her again. When I arrived, we did some reds. Reds for the unlearned are barbiturates-based sleeping pills ... or 'downers.' Needless to say, I got a little sloppy, and Bridgette was either gone or had no interest in me that night because I ended up driving twenty-five miles down the hill into Tustin, where Danny lived.

My mind was under the impression I was driving just fine until the police car lit the light bar behind me. So, I pulled over ... and for once, I wasn't belligerent ... I cooperated with his every request.

The cop took me through the sobriety test. My performance was pretty good. He almost agreed, "I am on the fence, but I will let you go if you park the truck and walk home." It was five miles back to Danny's, and the only thing that came to mind was getting the truck back in time.

"I cannot do that."

"Well, park the truck or go to jail."

"But I can't." He looked confused.

I was such an asshole back then; he should have booked me right then and there. He was being very cool and I was stoned and stupid but insistent.

"Okay, here is the deal. I am going to follow you home, and you better not exceed 10 mph. Any faster, you go straight to jail."

To this day, I have no idea the reasoning behind my decision. I had to have been on another planet … looping through town … high as a kite … with a police escort … really?

The five miles went quickly. I parked in front of Danny's house, locked the truck, waved to the cop, and went inside. Needless to say, the whole house went on alert for the police raid. They grabbed all of the dope and flushed everything down the toilet, then waited as I stepped inside.

"What?" I snapped.

"Where are the cops," They asked.

"Oh, they left … he was just making sure I got home safe with the truck. … Why?"

Call an Ambulance and Find a Bridge!

My first job came as a shock. One day I am getting $220 a month from Jack to stay in school, and the next day, I am punching a time clock. I had picked a photo major at one Junior College because I wanted to transfer from another Junior College and needed a class that the school didn't offer. The photography major was for no other reason than getting a transfer from one school to another. But it got me a job by accident.

Juanita worked at a bank, and when I dropped out of school, she freaked out. I did too. I was going to end up living under a bridge, and Juanita, being a concerned parent (finally), started asking people who came into the bank if they knew where I could find a job. One day, a guy who ran a printing facility came in and told Juanita, "If he knows a camera, maybe I can hire him." I interviewed, and the following Monday, I started my forty-year career. My only break was one year off serving as a bartender.

My first day on the job, I sat in my car with a sack lunch and cried … yep, I actually felt sorry for myself. The job entailed making plates for printing presses. Eventually, my mood changed. I was making $140 a week with the overtime, taxes were about 15%, gas was maybe 50 cents a gallon, and my rent was $50 bucks a month. Life was actually pretty good. I had a dog, a horse, a car, and some money in my pocket. In a matter of a few weeks, I moved into a good position because another guy took an extended vacation. Another young guy was hired, and we actually drove the plant. We prepped and plated everything for the presses, and we were organized. We cleaned the department and liked what we did. However, our stint fell short when Larry, the guy who had quit, returned. What a nitwit. A very bossy nitwit who was put in charge of the department Jay and I just revitalized. It ran seamlessly every day until Larry came back. He just kept pushing the window of tolerance; all he did for sure was piss us off. One day, he yelled at me. I ignored his command, and he raised his voice. I lost it.

I walked over to Big Frank, the cigar-smoking shop production manager. "You should call an ambulance because either Larry or me is going to need a ride."

"Go wait in my office."

When he came back, I had a new position in the bindery, far away from this Larry guy. Jay quit, and the department was never the same.

Life was good again in the cutting and folding department. Then I found out the new manager had hired a guy to do my old plate-making job for more money. I was pissed.

I had just worked a year, and with one small raise, I was still making less than the new guy. My emotions took control over my life back then.

I immediately went to the main building and marched into the manager's office, "What do you need?" he asked.

"Well, for a ham sandwich, I would throw you through that window. Fortunately for you, I am not hungry."

After my tirade, I walked out of his office and back to work. A few minutes later, the cigar-smoking production manager walked in, "I don't know what you did, kid, but I gotta fire you."

And that was it ... the end of my first ever real job. I knew it would end with me living under a bridge.

A Sister of Sorts

Before the story continues, you need some context. At the print shop where I was fired, there was a girl my age whom I was informed to stay away from when I first came to work there. My memory gets vague but I know the 'stay away' had to do with her being engaged. I believe her name was Sydney.

It's true that one action unveils an extensive course of events. Most of the people you meet are people at work. At the time, I was unattached and living in a little house on Fred and Jane's ranch. Somehow, that girl and I became friends and started drinking together. I think her engagement was canceled because of her soon-to-be husband's behavior. In fact, we were quite the drinkers. One night, while drinking, another guy tried to hang out with us but got violently ill and puked into his glass while sitting at a bar table with us. We were shocked and barely old enough to even be in the bar. After freaking out, we left the bar, but I am fairly certain we did not take him home.

It did not take long, and we did become great friends. We could talk about anything. She lived with her very rich parents on Balboa Island. However, their behavior was completely fucked up. I do remember her parents being icy cold to each other like they never kissed or touched one another. Although she and I had the occasional tumble in the sheets, this was not the basis of our friendship. I know that sounds made up, but that is the truth. A perfect example is one night, while I was asleep, I heard someone come inside. I never locked my doors. With my dog, Beethoven, who needs doorbells? The noise did wake me up. But before I could get up, she walked into my room and slipped into my bed.

She whispered, "Shhhh, go back to sleep. I just need to be close to you for a while."

I felt her snuggle up, and we both went back to sleep like two lonely souls in a rare moment of peace.

The next morning, she explained her parents had made love, and it freaked her out. And she needed to be close to me. She drove 45 minutes to get to my house that night. We were not lovers, but our relationship went on for years. It sounded weird, but it was more like a brother and sister from different parents. I loved her ... still do.

One night, while we were getting ready to go out for dinner and some dancing, she said, "I am either gay or bisexual. Please take me to this girl's bar on Garden Grove Blvd."

"Okay. But can we get dinner first?" She shrugged.

Our dinner was rushed, but after we arrived, she begged me to go inside. I was the only guy there and the vibe in the bar seemed alarming. It was downright cold. The feeling became so overwhelming that I could not even drink my beer.

A few minutes later, I grabbed her, "I will be in the car; it seems safer."

About an hour later, she came out to my car and said, "You can go home; I'll be fine." "Fine?" We kissed our last kiss, and I drove away.

She spent the next decade with a woman I never got to meet. After I got married, we remained friends and even went to lunch sometimes. Then, after my divorce, she came to my house and brought a girlfriend. The next day, she called and said, "The girl, Candis, from last night wants to go out with you."

The next night, she cooked dinner and invited me over. It was actually the beginning of a torrid two-year affair with her friend.

She and I are still friends. We speak once in a while. She is still gay, has lived with the same person, and worked at the same place forever. A very stable person indeed ... go figure. Although you could not say we are close, for that would be a matter of interpretation.

175

I think we will always actually remember our love ... no matter our distance. I know I will.

If One is Good ...

Nothing in my life was ever 'sort of.' It's just not my style. So, to finish the thought ... if one is good, then two is better. The first time after quitting smoking over twenty-three years ago, but who's counting, I started riding a bike. The last thing I wanted was to gain weight, but I did not want to exercise either. It just seemed that keeping my hands busy was the best option. So, to pass the time, I yoyo'd. Nevertheless, what does that have to do with weight loss and yo-yos? It must have some connection.

Each morning, I rode one loop in the park repeatedly. It was a good workout. But my ride was a 5-speed Schwinn beach cruiser, and I quickly grew out of it. Money at the time was tight, so buying a new bike stretched my bank account. However, I took the chance. I figured the money saved on smokes for one year would pay for the bike. In town, the local bike shop had a Marin 18-speed mountain bike. What a nice ride. So, I decided to start riding early, and I rode the bike trails. The first trail was 3 miles, which led me to 5 miles, and finally landed on 20 miles. I learned the names of everyone who ran, walked, or rode that trail in the early morning ... it was a family. Once I got my footing, so to speak, I started riding off-road. However, getting to the gate outside the State Park was a torturous hill. Before long, the hill became just a warm-up.

Saturday morning, a local group rode all over, and I quickly joined their group. Although I was not the fastest, my uphill skills took over.

Once, I was chugging up this hell's hill, dripping sweat, when this guy in his front yard asked, "Why are you doing this?"

"Because I enjoyed biking."

I guess sitting around stagnating wasn't my thing. So, on Sunday mornings, it was a game of golf. I'd tee off at 6 am, walk 18 holes carrying clubs, shoot mid-80s, and be done by 10:30 am. After taking an hour's nap, I hit the bike trails. My Sunday rides went about twenty-five miles to the beach and back. The ride took me to an ice cream shop on the way back. Granted, this wasn't an everyday event, but it illustrates my height of insanity. Driven was an understatement. I survived on salads and cycling. Later in life, it was running with the same commitment.

One day, a client asked, "Are you physically sick?"

"No, why?"

"If you are not sick, you need a hamburger and fries. And a vanilla shake!"

178

I went out that day and had a hamburger, some fries, and a vanilla shake!!! I've been eating like that ever since.

As all good things do, this, too, had to come to an end. I was out on the mountain bike one morning and riding with a very fast and fit group.

After about two hours, they were throwing their bikes over a barbed wire fence, "I'll see you later...I'm out."

They disappeared down the hillside. I laid down in the grass and rested. But a light went on ... I could catch them if I hurried ... so over the fence went my bike, and I flew down the hill. I looked up to find my riding buddies when my bike hit something.

My instincts kicked in quickly; I pulled both brakes lightly to slow my speed. The problem was my front wheel hit the dirt first and I rotated over the front bearing and shot out like a cannon. Needless to say, this whole mishap took less than a second or two.

When I finally knew I had to do something, I tried to get up. Each time I tried to get up, I would wake up in the dirt again. It did not take much longer before real fear took over, and I actually thought I might die.

So, I swear to God ... I used a stick and wrote a note in the dirt to my family, "I am not happy."

At that moment, the serenity prayer came to mind. *God grant me the serenity to accept the things I cannot change, the courage to change the things I can, and the wisdom to know the difference.* I love these words because a second later, the thought came to mind: yell, help, you, dummy!

"Hhhhheeeelllllppp."

I was on the side of a hill; it was getting late, and I had not heard or seen anyone since regaining consciousness

A few seconds later, I swear someone answered. "Okay."

In a few minutes, another biker below me in the valley heard my call (cry) and rode up and found me. I stood up and he looked at me.

"Your collarbone is broken. Hang on, I'll go find a ranger."

And just like that, a ranger stuffed me and my bike in his jeep and took me all the way to the hospital.

The emergency room doctor took one look at me, "Get him a room."

The nurse cut my shirt off and said, "Now, what's wrong with this picture?"

"Come stand a little closer," I replied.

"Why?"

"Cause I am going to throw up all over you."

The doctor heard me and laughed, "Get him something for the pain and nausea."

Later, he told me it was a high-impact shatter, and I needed to see a bone doctor in the morning.

Now, this was not the worst pain. That is held for the head-on collision on my motorcycle with an '89 Lincoln, and that was not even close!

Needless to say, it took over a year to recover, and it changed my life significantly. I became mortal for the first time and still sleep on my right side. But some things never change, as I still obsess over all things good.

One Thing Leads to Another

The LA Harley Davidson Motorcycle riders were a pretty cool group. When they saw my '03 Springer in LA, I became an automatic member. I tried attending one of their meetings ... but I have to be truthful ... I ain't no biker ... at least not a club rider. However, they did teach me a few things.

One morning, we stopped for breakfast at a little mountain restaurant, and everyone left their jackets on the bikes.

I asked, "Aren't you worried about someone stealing them?"

The point man on this ride looked at me, "No one fucks with a dozen bikes, my friend.

"Cool by me."

Later that day, we stopped at another bar; everyone was drinking and getting loud. In case you didn't figure it out by now, I don't drink, so I was just hanging around waiting to ride again. They were talking about this wild party in the desert with thousands of people that lasted a week. I took a mental note and forgot about it ... for then.

About a week later, I ran into my good friend and fellow biker ... Monty ... at an AA meeting. I told him about the ride and mentioned the party.

He lit up "The Burning Man." I was lost.

"What is the Burning Man?"

The revelation was enlightening. I was fifty-one and had no knowledge of this event.

He just said, "Go to burningman.com, and you'll see."

My research shocked me. I read this section called "Tales of The Playa." The stories were from people who just experienced the event and went home to write about their experience.

The Burning Man is all about sharing. Finally, I have found my long-lost brothers and sisters at the Burning Man. I bought a ticket.

A couple of weeks later, Monty was at the meeting. Needless to say, my excitement overflowed. I grabbed my ticket and pushed it across the table.

"So, you are going?"

I always wanted to go, but being a teacher, I had to work. However, being retired, I am going too.

We agreed to caravan with our 'biker rule' in play. It was a simple rule that no one owes anything to anyone. You ride together or go separate ways whenever.

No questions asked. Our three-month planning period worked great, but the technical details were not important. However, I will tell you about the great gifts we brought.

The fact that my talents as a painter are not great doesn't matter. I'd been carrying around an idea for years of something to paint. So, no matter my talents, I decided to paint anyway.

And Sebbe always said, "Everyone is an artist; they just paint in different ways."

But the more I thought about my idea, the more it seemed boring. How in the world would anyone experience anything while watching me fuck up a canvas. Although, here is the cool thing. It turns out I am creative. I just can't sing or paint. But I conceived the 'Painting Wall'. I built it, took it apart, and stored it so I'd know how to put it back together again on the playa. And that was my gift. Nine pre-stretched and framed canvases 4'x4' attached to a wooden frame with all the paints and brushes you could need.

I put it together on the playa. I set up the tables with all the tools and turned on the lanterns at night to keep it open for everyone who passed to stop and paint ... with me! My gift gave me great joy.

Monty built an evaporating shower ... but I did not fully appreciate how cool and important it was going to be. When we got there, he set it up, and the next day, we showered in it, and it rocked. Then the wind blew our curtains down, so it became a neighborhood curtainless shower, and a ton of beautiful girls showered there every day. Nudity became the norm on the playa. Not that I was nude or that everyone else was ... just that it did not matter one way or the other. The forbidden fruit was available, and that changed the equation of life. Like being 15 years old in London!

But there was more. Monty walked over to me with a shoebox full of glass necklaces he made. They were beautiful. We had about 500 of them that we gave away over the next week ... it was a gas. Necklaces and the Painting Wall ... our camp was a lot of fun!

A week later, we loaded up on a Sunday morning and headed home. The event made new friends, and we cried, hugged, and pushed on our own way. We stopped that morning in Sparks, Nevada, and had breakfast— our first good meal in a week. The hostess set us in the middle of the dining room. We were covered in playa dust, our hair was white, and we were draped in jewelry—even flashing earrings.

Our emotions were still running wild, and we wore sunglasses and ignored the other patrons. It was a shaky drive home, and at 9 pm, we stopped for fast food. We cried and hugged ... like never before, that night, our emotions were beyond control. We had just gone to the moon and were nearly home.

2003 was my first trip to Burning Man. Monty died a few short years later. Tonight ... as I remember that week ... the emotions flood my soul once again like it was yesterday. We might as well have been on the moon.

11

Young Guns

My family moved to Pocatello, Idaho—or actually Alameda, a suburb of Pocatello—in 1960. But you must understand we were on the edge of nowhere—and it was great!

Donnie, my best friend, and I were into making coaster race cars. So, we dragged it up this hill that bottomed out in front of a girl's house we both liked. Now, our decision to race down the hill was a huge mistake. How we did not die that afternoon is unbelievable.

Imagine this ... steep hill, no brakes, and hauling ass. After making it to the bottom, we got the car turned and were not smashed by any oncoming vehicles. So, a huge success. In light of our achievement, we made one with an electric motor. It worked with a cord, but it was too short.

Things were great with Donnie; we had many adventures until his life pivoted. His father died in a car accident on the way home from a hunting trip. Donnie just kind of vanished, weird, but that is life.

As with most kids, I moved on to new friends. Leonard became my new best friend. All the kids slept out a lot during that summer ... the nights were warm, and the town was way safe.

One night, we decided to play 'Catch the Whistler.' We met in the afternoon to prepare. We never did catch whoever it was that was whistling and moving over and over. It was fun chasing them, though. We slept outside one night and stayed up late until the girls across the street fell asleep in their tent. The plan combined putting a sprinkler inside the tent, turning it on, and running like hell. Needless to say, the screaming woke their parents, and they were pissed. But we laughed ourselves to sleep.

Once, we organized a baseball game. We mixed up a bunch of kids of different ages. I was nine, weighed about fifty pounds, and played shortstop. One of the kids could hit like a pro, and he launched a line drive right at me. My instinct forced me to turn my head, but I took it right in the temple. It knocked me right out. I probably got a concussion with that one. But back then, we played on; it was just growing up.

In Idaho, snow comes with the start of school. So, with that weather in mind, we convinced Juanita to let us hold the car bumper and drag us to school. We called it hooky bobbing. And it was assuredly dangerous. When someone pointed out it was illegal, she made us ride the bus, so we used that bumper instead.

Another time at school, there was a young fourth grader who we called 'slow' in those days. I picked up and walked with him to school each day. He was cool, and I felt bad because some of the other kids were mean to him. Anyway, one morning, they picked a fight with him in the schoolyard. He was bigger than them, but he never fought back. They dragged him over to a snow pile and rubbed his face in it. I was furious and started to pull the other kids away.

"This is uncool," I said. They laughed at me. When they finally quit, I helped him up.

I remember the tears in his eyes. I felt bad and always hoped he would kick their asses someday. He had the size, just not the smarts.

One day after school, I decided to walk home with a girl from my grade. However, my personality got me in trouble again when I started talking about how I could beat up her brother. The message soon got relayed to him, and before I knew what happened, he was standing directly in front of me with nowhere to escape. I freaked and ran; however, behind me was a hill that was straight up and full of snow. Needless to say, it did not stop my assailant. He tackled me from behind. But I don't remember it hurting; most likely, it was from the heavy winter coats, and he did not hit me in the face.

After much recovery, someone might learn their lesson from antagonizing other people, but not me ... again my mouth got me in deep trouble. We were having our only hot lunch all year—hot dogs in the gym. The entire school was thrilled. I must have been out of control because the principal pulled me out of line, insisting I stand behind the door until he came and got me.

It might be amazing, but I actually followed orders. I stood behind the door for at least two hours ... lunch was over ... the cooks were gone ... the light turned off ... and yet no one missed me. Suddenly, I realized no one missed me. So, I darted out of the school and home, crying to Juanita. At times, my mother did show some concern for her children. We drove back to the school, and she bitch slapped that old man. The embarrassment became pretty clear.

The Eighth Grade

Juanita moved us to the beach in the middle of the eighth grade, which was fine with me because we spent an entire six months in Anaheim. It was a place that only a shrug could truly capture. Let's see ... I raced slot cars at the hobby shop ... Danny built them ... I drove them. We smoked cigarettes and lived in apartments. The Jewish kid across the way invited me in during the holidays, his family was nice. But for some reason, I thought blowing out the Hanukkah candles would be funny. They freaked, and I didn't understand. There was so much no one ever shared with me growing up.

Juanita, per usual, left us home alone a lot. One night, we heard someone walking around in the gravel behind our unit, so Danny said to me, "I have the shotgun loaded ... do you have the rifle ready to go?"

We hoped that would scare them away. It didn't; our drunken cousin Jerry had come for a place to crash. He was asleep on the couch when Aunt Juanita got home.

After getting sent home from school for smoking, we suddenly moved to Newport Beach. At first, it was great. I rode my bike down to the beach from the bluffs where we lived. Then I rode to the Fun Zone and took the ferry across to Balboa Island and home up the hill to the bluffs. It was raining the whole way, and I loved it all.

The school year started at the junior high. Before long, I was running with other 'parent-abandoned' children. Believe me, there were quite a few. We had parents but missed most of what was happening. For example, we'd sneak into the theater, open the bathroom windows, and let others come in for free. We drank beers under the bridge and rode our bikes everywhere.

The summer between eighth and ninth grade we were on the loose. During the daytime, we rode bikes and skateboards, plus took our surfboards to the beach on homemade rickshaws behind our bikes. Some days, we'd fill up our squirt guns and hang out in front of the Savon Drug Store. When a woman would walk out with packages in her hands, we would swoop in on our bikes and try to drown her on the spot. Then we would wheelie away on our Stingray bikes, laughing out loud. Before long, we got braver and started hanging out in front on foot. It was much easier to hit our victim. One day, just as our attack began, the store manager came running out and actually caught us. He shook us down, took our water weapons, and promised to call the police if we didn't stop. We moved on.

Now, we became experts at cruising past the soft drink trucks that parked in front of the grocery store and pulled bottles off on the fly. An easy score until one of our friend's brothers identified us. We were forced to turn ourselves in. Another shakedown, only this time, we had to mop the entire supermarket.

At night, we hung out at Family Billiards ... that was anything but 'family' friendly. We all had breakdown cues and could play a mean nine-ball. The place held a little different crowd ... a more serious set of thieves. One night, we cruised past a car, and a guy circled back to grab a purse from the unattended vehicle. There was a ton of money in it, so we divided it up. I was not comfortable and insisted we put the purse back and only take a few dollars ... they agreed ... and put the purse back, but later, I learned they kept all of the money.

One night, on the way to the pool hall we scored again ... only this time, I could not get behind this stealing thing ... I wasn't a thief then and am still not one today. Later that night, I woke Danny up ... he had the car ... "Hey, my buddies stole a purse today, and I know where they ditched it. I want to get it out of the dumpster and give it back. I just wanna put my share back and hope the owner finds it.

"Agreed. Come on … "

It was after midnight, and it got more interesting by the minute. I dug through the dumpster and found her purse, and they left everything except the money. I scrambled out and put my share back in while Danny drove me to the spot where I wanted to leave it. I placed the purse on the sidewalk inside the apartment complex and ran back, climbed in, and we sped away.

It did not make things right, but it made me feel better. I am no thief … the karma got me every time, anyway. Anytime I stole something, something bad would happen. Once, I stole a bike for the night, and the next morning, my surfboard was gone … instant karma, hey.

Years later, Danny and I were talking about the night I returned the purse, and he laughed, "Hey after you went to sleep, I went back and took the money." The question remains: did he really? I think he did.

It was also the summer of love. All the families on the beach came with teenage girls. We scored. Although, scoring at fourteen is much different than being an adult. But when summer ended, we all went on with life as if nothing ever happened. One of the guys who took all the money that first night later went to prison for robbing a jewelry store. I have only seen one other guy since that summer, 47 years ago. Too bad really. But we were all transient.

The Movie is Over

The idea of risking jail time in a foreign country did not seem appealing. On December 30th, 1969, my life abroad came to a screeching halt. So, leaving of my own volition had to happen. However, my initial move to London was due to serious trouble with the law, so coming back for the same reason was not surprising.

It should not be shocking that I drank all the way home on the plane, even though I was underage. It had something to do with international law. It seems that eighteen is the magic age. Later in the airport, I bought Juanita a bottle of cheap Vodka; back then, all I knew about was Smirnoff. If my memory serves me, I think I had a guitar, and I know I had long hair.

After the plane landed and I got off, I had to walk up to police security. He took one look at me and said, "Right this way." I followed him to a checkpoint.

The cop proceeded to take my luggage apart, double-checking everything. After he was convinced there was no contraband in my bag, he let me go. I was actually uninterested in his actions as I was as clean as it gets ... so my attention drifted to the guy in the line next to me. He had this rather large cardboard box all tied up and taped shut.

"What's in the boxes?" They asked.

"Art Statues," he said.

When they ordered him to open the box, he looked really nervous. "Step aside," he did.

The guard pulled a pocket knife and cut the tape. Then, they started pulling out statues. The agents began inspecting, weighing two at a time. He stuck to his story; he collected art. Of course, this was back in the day when rights were rights. They had no evidence to refute his claim.

But I am telling you. The statues had hash molded into the castings. All the agents knew it as well, but with no evidence, they had to let him go. Any other action could be viewed as an invasion of privacy and destruction of personal property if they were wrong. They told him to pack it up and go on his way. To this day, I can still hear him sigh.

Once I hit the States, the customs agent said I could keep the Vodka, but under no circumstances should I try to bring in alcohol while underage. No problem, I won't be making this trip again ... for a long, long time. After I got to Juanita's apartment, needless to say, I drank some Vodka. She looked confused but did not say a word.

It did not take long to reconnect with the old neighborhood. I found the same people doing the same things. My high school buddy was still around, and we rented a house in Laguna Beach. In days, my life was right back into the world of drugs, alcohol, and everything that went along.

My next step was to find Pamela, my girlfriend, but knowing the crowd, finding her was pretty easy. In a dark, needle-ridden dump, she was shooting heroin with a bad group. It pissed me off; however, trying to rescue her was a bust. Instead, she was hooked on BB King and nodding with the boys. Our special connection turned dark, so talking about why it didn't work would be useless. We were able to spend some time together and have fun, but nothing seemed balanced. I actually liked the downers because it was the only way to cope with her crowd.

One night, we were hanging out and getting stoned when we decided to go to the movies. I had no idea what we went to see, but it was the old theater in downtown Laguna Beach. I do remember it being a very small crowd, so we went up to the balcony and hid as far back as possible. We dozed off, but when we woke, the theater was dead silent. I listened for a few moments

... not a sound to be heard. I woke her, and she whispered, "What is going on?"

I said, "It's 3:30 in the morning ... they closed the place down and went home ... they never saw us up here."

"What are we going to do?" she asked.

In the back of my mind, this wasn't cool. "We are going downstairs and exit through the crash door. Then straight to the car and driving home."

She grabbed my hand and nodded.

I kicked the crash bar ... no bells or sirens, just silence. If there was an alarm, we only had a few minutes to disappear, so we vanished in a hurry.

Yes, we laughed about it later ... but what else are you going to do? I lost track of her shortly after that. I knew she was still using the bad boys, and there was no way to get her out. Many years later, I heard she got married to a guy and had four kids. Today, she might be a grandmother living in Maui or something else cool. Who knows. :)

Snake Bit

On Memorial Day weekend in 1978, I thought things were pretty good. My wife was five months pregnant with our first child, and we were heading to the desert for the weekend with our business partners and their two boys. Our hotel ended up being in the middle of nowhere. A small town, if you will, called Desert Ironwoods. It was Friday morning, and I was determined to have fun. We checked in and moved our gear upstairs. It felt like nothing could crawl in bed with you on the second floor.

The place had twelve rooms and a pool, nothing more, nothing less. Once we unloaded the buggy and motorcycles off the trailer where the camp was situated, it was drinking time.

Leonard said, "Let's go shoot my guns?"

Everyone said, "OK."

Pretty soon, we were firing away at bottles we set up. We kept missing, and the bullets were ricocheting off the rocks. I have said before I am not comfortable with real guns, particularly large handguns. Maybe it was a past life thing. So, our shooting didn't last long, mainly because of the ricocheting.

The night was a typical night in the desert. All I wanted to do was drink and go cruising in the desert with the dune buggy, but it was only a two-seater, so I couldn't escape for long. My wife did not enjoy the sand car, the desert, the booze, the pool, or the pot. She was just never happy in the desert.

After dinner, we were all hanging out in our room, planning an early morning ride, when Leonard got up and headed out, barefoot, to the truck to get his helmets and boots for the morning ride. A few moments later, he came back, racing into the room, slammed against the wall. We turned and looked; it was unusual behavior. Next thing, he was sitting on the floor with his foot bleeding.

"Hey, I think something bit me."

It did look as though someone hit his big toe with a sledgehammer. Needless to say, we all freaked. I took off downstairs to figure out what bit him. That was stuuuupid!!! Fortunately, I did not run into a sidewinder rattler. Leonard's wife was the only one remaining calm.

We were all standing above him, sitting on the floor, "Guys, I do not want to die tonight?" They could be deadly.

My wife looked at me and said, "You have to get him to the ER right away." I quickly sobered up.

His wife was really freaked out, and we lost track of the kids. I said I was driving him to the closest hospital. That was Brawly, at least an hour away. It was decided. I take my V8 Camaro with the snake-bit friend in the back seat and his wife in the front. In seconds, the race was on.

On the way, we stopped at the Sherriff's house in Ocotillo Wells to ask for help, but the old fucker flat-out admitted he wasn't a cop. His only option was to put ice on the bite and drive. I fired up the V8, and off we flew. Driving was something I could do!

We hit Highway 86 and really started to roll. I went through two small towns at 90mph, laying on the horn, and for the first time, I wanted to be pulled over as we needed a police escort.

But, of course, not a cop in sight ... his wife was sitting next to me, crying, "Please, Thomas, slow down."

By that time, I hit 100 mph, passing everyone in sight. My buddy asked his wife to please shut up and let him drive.

The car was dark, but Leonard's foot was the size of a football now. Unfortunately, the poison was traveling to his heart, causing his foot to turn blue.

We finally hit Brawley on a Memorial Day weekend. The streets were packed, jammed up with rigs pulling toys. Then, just ahead, I noticed the hospital sign pointing right. But the left turn lane was empty, so I hooked it hard on the green light, spun around the traffic, and made a right turn.

My tires squealed, sending smoke all over behind me. Nothing else mattered. I ignored the traffic, hoping they just got out of the way cause I didn't want to hit them ... and by the way ... still no cops ... what the fuck!

We literally flew into the hospital parking lot, and they were waiting for us outside with a gurney. I slammed on the brakes and did a 4-wheel drift right up to them. Leonard was 37 years old ... apparently, they thought I was bringing in a 67-year-old. Age makes a difference.

The hotel manager, Len, found and killed the snake. It was ten feet from where we were all running around. It was hiding in the sand next to my van tire. Len called ahead to the hospital, confirming it was a sidewinder. They loaded Leonard on the gurney and rolled him to the emergency room. They immediately injected him with painkillers, and believe me, he was in pain.

A few seconds later, he started turning colors, getting very sick. "Has he been drinking?"

"Hell, yes ... he has been drinking all fucking day."

They panicked.

Now, he was suffering from alcohol and barbiturate poisoning on top of a heavy dose of neurological snake venom. The staff rolled him into the elevator, and we didn't see him again for four days. His room was next to the psych ward, and later, he swore he heard them crying and screaming as he passed in and out of consciousness.

They saved his vital organs with anti-venom in both legs. It took eight weeks of intensive therapy to recover. Now, Leonard limps every Memorial Day. He won a small lawsuit from the hotel but gave me half the driver's fees, I guess. However, not too long after, he stole me blind at the office and moved away, leaving me to pick up the pieces at the shop. It took me three years to right the ship and then dump it.

After the incident, he moved to Northern California. I did have a curious moment and looked him up. Not much had changed, but he had turned grey. :) We made amends; nevertheless, it could have never been the same.

Because I Own Him ...

It's hard to admit at times, but I have never been a 'good parent.' The whole separation thing about friends and parents, making decisions that were not up for debate. We are good friends and will always be there for my two kids, but it is what it is. Although, they understand much more about my life.

When Bret was sixteen and fully engaged in the whole high school thing, he came home and casually mentioned going camping on the beach with friends. Since I knew all the beach kids, I agreed without hesitation.

His mother looked at me, "No, Bret, I don't think so ... you're not going to drink beer all night with a bunch of older guys."

Bret jumped up, "Why not?"

To say the least, he was very upset but knew the battle was already lost. Jillian, his little sister, was six ... she was her mother's mime ... so before anyone else could answer Bret's objection, she said, "Because I said so ..."

"Tell her to shut up!" he walked away.

Another time, while at work, a friend called to inform me the west swell was hitting Blackies (Newport

Pier) and the offshore winds were awesome. He was going to grab him some.

It was about 10 am, the kids were in school, "Sounds good. We'll meet you there." I replied.

I left the office, grabbed the boards and wetsuits, and drove to Bret's school. Oh, he was in the eighth grade. I walked into the office and asked if someone could get him out of class; he would be coming with me. A moment later, the vice principal came out and asked, "Why I was taking him out of school."

I didn't even think, but his question pissed me off.

"Because I own him. Please hurry ... we need to leave immediately."

If you have ever been pulled from class by the vice principal, you can understand Bret's concern when he walked into the office until he saw me. We walked out the door and climbed in the van ... the boards were on top. :)

I had surfboards made for Bret once in a while, and when I would bring a new one home, his mother would point out that I could not give him an expensive toy because it was Tuesday. I claimed they were tools ... she wasn't laughing. Eventually, I started sneaking into the garage and hiding them in his board bag and putting the old one in the rafters. She would always make a point to let me know she knew.

The day after Bret turned sixteen and got his driver's license, we went car shopping, but his mother was sick and unable to come along, which was good for Bret! We came home with a very well-priced Toyota mini truck. It was used ... very low mileage ... a lift kit, a big chrome wheel ... and a stick shift. He was in heaven ... I was stoked.

We eventually put a shell on the back and had AC installed. When he was eighteen and in college, he wanted a "car" instead of a truck. I was okay, but his mother was livid that I would even consider buying him another car.

She was serious, "No, if he wants a car, then he can buy it himself."

A couple of weeks later, she went out of town for something. I bought aftermarket wheels for the Honda Civic he wanted. We put them in the back of his truck and drove to the Honda dealer. Two hours later, he drove off the lot with a brand-new black-on-black EX Civic ... with the Hockenhiemer wheels and 40 series radials. Next, it was off to the suspension shop to be lowered, then to the muffler shop for pipes, and finally to the sound shop for the trunk system and speakers.

This was one badass car. His mother was soooooo pissssssed. It was weeks until she said anything to me beyond the absolute minimum.

He and his friends would climb in that car, turn up the sound system, and, as he put it, they would bump on out.

Once, I found used beer bottles in the trunk, "What the fuck?"

"It was my turn to clean the party house."

"Then why the fuck didn't you throw them away?" He just laughed.

I should have paid more attention to that beer bottle discovery because a few weeks later, he was arrested for driving under the influence. Whether he was or not is unimportant ... the damage was done. He lost his license for 14 months.

"I told you so ..." his mother snapped.

I sold the badass car, and he rode a train to and from college ... when he got his license back, I bought him another Civic ... not new, but still!

Like I said ... I was more of a friend than a parent, but things have worked out ... he finished school ... got a great degree in Biology ... a great job he still has ...

married a great girl, and they are soon to be parents for the first time. So ... will he be a parent or a friend? Or both?

12

Upward Basketball

One year, while on a hiking trip, my wife volunteered me to coach a basketball team in a church league. Jillian played a little ball; it surprised me, but I did not mind the coaching thing. However, I learned I had to lead practice with a weekly testimonial. A missionary who helped me - made a deal. He'd do the testimonials before games and practices, and I do the coaching. Actually, we became good friends. Plus, he was a surfer who took surfboards to third-world countries for children. I loaned him my board bags ... things worked out.

The team was really fun ... they were about 8 years old, and none of them could shoot a basket or even understand the gameplay. So, I got one of the neighborhood girls (Nickie), who played on the high school JV basketball team, to help me. She got some school credit and accepted. It was amazing; she helped with the first game, and before long, they were shooting, dribbling, scoring, and winning.

I never left my chair during the games ... the youth sport with Bret taught me a lesson. Nicki and I would sit together as they ran up and down the floor, yelling constant reminders to them ... particularly to keep their hands up.

The other coaches, for some reason, thought we had the worst team. When we were sitting at 4 and 0, the heat turned up ... ah yes ... the air of success ... even in an eight-year-old church league girls' basketball, the competition between the dads was alive and well ... it is true ... as my friend Bruce used to say, "Everything wrong with the world began in Little League baseball!"

The rules in this league were a little different. The clock ran continuously. Four eight-minute periods, it never stopped, though ... for injury on anything. However, the substitution rules were very cool. Each player had a number related to their ability—1 being the best and 8 being not the best. The substitutions were made every period based on a mathematical equation— it was science, and it defeated coaches' attempts to underplay or hide their lower numbers.

We finally met up with the undefeated 'team to beat.' The coach was a younger guy who supposedly had a great team. Before the game started, I felt it was important to tell Nicki to be on her best behavior. The

211

game started, we played well, even scored, plus, defended and everything was fine. In fact, we gave them a run for their money. At the end of the third quarter, we were ahead by two points.

The other team was comfortable … they had a better set of girls than ours (theoretically) coming out in the fourth period.

I leaned over, "Nicki if we happen to score first, you will actually see some smoke come from their coach's ears."

"Really?"

We both smile and settle in for the final 8-minute run. The missionary's daughter immediately stole the ball from the other team's best player, who was expected to carry them to victory. She steals the ball … throws it upcourt, and bingo … we score first. The other coach is running up and down the court … screaming orders.

Nicki and I yelled, "Move … move, move!"

We traded points for the next few minutes while time ran out. We were still in the lead. The other coach is melting down but finally crosses the line. The referee halted play. Not the clock, just the play, asking the coach to settle down.

He stopped yelling but pleaded, "Let them play, just let them play!!!"

The referees refused to let play restart because of the coach's behavior, so the clock expired, and we won 5 and 0, baby. After that, we seemed to relax, but we lost a couple on the way home and ended up at six and two.

We may not have been the best overall, but I can assure you we all had smiles. The girls learned some valuable life lessons, and I managed to forge a relationship with the missionary. In the end, I lead the testimonial.

Death Drop

Just as life seemed to settle, my wife divorced me ... asked me to move. Our son was somewhere around three; it felt pretty devastating.

In my mind at the time, who really cares anymore about right and wrong ... she was serious. My anger got the better of me for many years. I came dangerously close, falling off the edge again.

I was a hard worker, a somewhat successful guy, about thirty-one. Did I drink every day ... yes. Did I smoke weed every day ... yes. Did I work 12 hours every day ... yes. Did we have any money ... not really. But my father had just given each of his kids this stock he owned for many years. At the time he started transferring, it was worth about $120,000 in 1981 (or so ... I can't put the exact years together anymore); that was a lot of money.

I came home shortly after, "Let's buy a house?"

She replied, "I want a divorce."

So, I stormed out, with her blessing, and took all of the stock money.

The incident drove me into a deep depression. I could hardly work and cried all the time. I was in love and wanted to raise my son.

Since my life fell apart, I moved back to the canyon of my youth. My drug use escalated while the bar was literally across the street, which meant I crawled home every night after drinking all day. And, for a few months, I held up in that little house ... barely held my shop together (I owned half of a small printing shop) and found solace in vodka and cocaine.

My very good friend kept trying to get me to come down the hill and hang out ... I was not interested. Then, one day, he called and said his wife's father's daughter was in town ... she was hot and looking for someone to party with—
I was the one.

"You have to go out with her," he argued. "OK ... OK ... I'll go."

I met her that Friday night at my friend's house. We did go out, but you know we ended up at my little canyon hideaway, and we had a great evening.

The experience kicked me in the butt. It woke me up ... I remember looking in the mirror the next day, and there was this face with a curly, untrimmed beard. My eyes were blurry, and I had long, stringy hair and horrible dark circles. Before long, I found myself in a nice, small place on the beach. It had a boat deck, hot tub, and deck.

Perfect. I could run with the beautiful people, so I started drinking at nice places. The nice little outboard-powered 15-foot boat that looked like I stole it from Disneyland was cool. The girl's name escapes me, but she hung around. We had some great times ... yes, I shaved, cut my hair, and cared more about my appearance. However, I almost never saw my son.

On the weekend, I had this desert spot where we went with the sand rail, drank, and raced. I invited my new girlfriend ... she accepted. So, we went shopping to buy her proper clothes. We drove out to my special place and drank all night, then got high—all the things you do in the desert. It was insane, of course, and dangerous to boot. The next morning, we started with Brandy Alexanders and joints to get the day going. We hopped in the buggy, stopped to gas up ... threw some drinks in the cooler, and left for a day in the dunes.

I took her everywhere ... been to all the places many times. We finally came to Devil's Slide. It was a dangerous little spot, but I had been up and down it a hundred times.

My goal included giving her a thrill. The hillside was several stories high, so I crept up to the top from the back, eased my way over the rocks, and gunned the motor; over we went. As soon as we crested, the front dropped right out from under us ... I snapped awake and immediately realized we had jumped off the wrong point. The buggy went airborne. The whole car pointed almost straight down, and the wheels were barely making contact with the sand ... barely. I remember everything crystal clear ... like a slow motion fuck up. My worst fears flashed before me. I just knew the back was going to rotate over our heads and throw us into an end-over-end cartwheel down the face. The only thing I could think of was keeping my foot off of the pedals while my hands crushed the steering wheel. My passenger just kept screaming; however, it could not have been from fear since she had no idea what was happening. I was frozen ... beyond the drinks I shouldn't have had ... and completely immersed in total fear.

And then just like that, it was over ... the front wheels touched down, and back wheels hit the sand ... we bottomed out ... the suspension was compressed to the stops ... I hit the accelerator to pull it out of the rebound, and we flared out into the flats, where I pulled the turning brake and spun us sideways and to a halt.

She burst into laughter, "Let's do it again."

I was numb ... she had no idea what the last few seconds had defined ... life or death. I was exhausted, but I do not remember anything after that about the desert that weekend. I took her home but never let on like we were in danger. It was all in a day in the desert. We never went back there. She was looking for someone else, not me. She liked boys but loved girls. And it didn't matter; I had the beach house and the business, and the depression was gone temporarily. I just kept rolling. I was headed for the last house on the block. I just didn't understand it at the time, but my life was in a death drop, too!

London Robin Moon

At seventeen, I was in London with Jack at my summer family. It rained all the time, but we lived in Highgate. The story of how I met Robin is a mystery. However, this I know ... she was smoking hot, and to this day, I can see her smile ... her face is inches from mine. The memory goes as far as seeing her front teeth. They were not perfect ... in fact, one slightly overlapped the other ... her eyes were alive and matched her smile. She had dirty blond hair at shoulder length, and her bangs were cut just above her eyes. And the funny part was she really liked me. I think she was nearly seventeen ... I totally think I loved her.

Robin, her mother and brother lived around the corner ... if I could only remember what they were doing there ... it had to be winter or maybe spring ... but the rain was cold that day. Somehow, I found her, and we slipped off to be alone. We found a warm, dry spot in her garage and immediately wrapped ourselves up together. I was young and eager; my hands wandered across her lovely body; she was loving every moment ... maybe even more than me. Then something happened ... maybe we just knew we had to stop ... and that was that ... we came out of the garage and went our separate ways.

And I still cannot remember anything, but these three facts ... first, her mother was wonderful ... a real loving parent ... this confused me ... she seemed to embrace everything about her children ... not just who they were. Second ... her brother ... who was just slightly older than me ... played the guitar ... not just OK ... but really OK ... and he could sing like an angel ... I remember wishing to have that ability. His hair was 1969 long and curly. And the third thing I remember for sure was that their family was sort of international. Robin went to a private American school in Geneva, Switzerland. Her brother was similarly engaged in an upscale school somewhere ... and he performed occasionally.

Maybe they were all famous ... I would not know ... I just fell in love with Robin. And suddenly, it was the summer of 1969, and I left home ... for good. But lived on the streets ... sort of ... with Scbbe and Dchilo, and we were gaming the music industry for a berth at the top. Somehow, Robin was back in town, and she found me ... don't know how ... but she, her mom and her brother were staying in the West End off of Bayswater Road. We were hanging out with them one summer afternoon ... and I think Sebbe and Dehilo were with us ... at their flat watching the TV. But I remember we were watching the landing on the moon (or maybe the landing on the fake moon in a secret studio somewhere!). Crazy but true.

Towards the end of summer, Sebbe, Dehilo, and I moved way north ... about twenty miles from the city. We were getting serious about our music adventure, and this was saving us some money ... what little we had. My hair was long and unkempt ... my clothes were ragged hip; I was skinny and dingy. We had this community phone, and somehow, Robin found me at that number and said she was coming to see me to say goodbye before she left for school. I gave her directions and promised to meet her at the bus stop. I have to keep saying this ... I do not know where I met her or how she kept finding me ... maybe through my dad ... but I will always wonder what finally happened to her.

She stepped off the bus, beautiful as ever ... she had everything going on. I could tell from her eyes she was shocked by my looks. And my personality had changed. I was quiet and sulky and didn't say much. I did not attempt to hold her, kiss her, or ask her for her phone number. I was just there; it was awkward. "I am going back to the city," she said. The next bus that stopped swept her up, and I watched her as she left forever. I am watching her disappear right now as I write this story. I was terrified and knew I was losing her forever.

I turned my back when her bus rounded the first corner. That was it; Robin was gone, and in a few short months, London would be, too.

The Old Man of Pop … Almost

I have mentioned this guy who called himself Sebbe many times. He was a lot of things … some of them good, and some of them downright hard to figure. When he walked into a room, his presence was felt. If you said the room went silent, you'd be close. He was only eighteen years old, yet he seemed like an old man. I wanted to say old soul, but I might laugh. The one thing he was for sure was a songwriter. He had a knack for putting little Buddhist land mines everywhere in his songs. His phrases were beyond exceptional, and his melodies were great.

One day, he ran an ad in the *London Financial Time*s in the personals section that received a lot of attention. It was a simple ad. All it said was, "Wanted, a Brian Epstein. We met an attorney named Tony, who had a friend named Derek, who was a retired ad executive.

Derek saw the ad and called Tony, "You have to call this guy; he is a genius."

So, we met with Tony and then with Tony and Derek. Derek lived in Hampstead Heath in north London, which, back then, was a very hip place. I am not sure how this all came about, but everyone was looking for easy money and the fast lane in the summer of 1969. Many agents and studios were willing to take a chance. The Beatles had just come out of nowhere and opened the floodgate. We were booked into a private studio in a private home that was also on the Heath.

Tony told Derek he arranged the studio for us, along with a pianist, a bass player, and a drummer. Plus, we got Tom, who ran the recording equipment. After we got acquainted, the drummer, who I cannot remember, was very ordinary. The pianist, who I'll never forget, was a washed-up blues musician. The bass player was a long-haired rocker, of whom he didn't have a clue. And then there was Tom, a very quiet and thorough recording technician. We talked about the songs, the vibe Sebbe was going for, and the lyrics. I strummed each song to help them focus.

On the first song, our drummer was immediately out of sync, the bass player went solo, and the pianist was drunk. Tom quietly started to take after take until none of us could stand it anymore. After that, we called Derek. We, the beggars, became the choosers. The conversation was simple. Get everyone out of the studio, but Tom is on the recording desk, or we are gone. In five minutes, the hired musicians packed up and left.

Soon, we started recording, and forty-five minutes later, we were done. I had strummed the songs, and Sebbe sang the lyrics. I think we reeled off six to seven tracks. Sebbe and I felt our performance was less than acceptable, but we accomplished something that day. Tony called and said, "I'll call you in a few days." It was going to be a long and dreadful few days. Neither Sebbie nor I (Tavoh was my stage name :) thought we stood a chance in hell.

The next day, we were doing nothing but wondering what would come next. Then, a neighbor knocked on the door and said we had a call on the communal phone. Needless to say, we were anxious. Apparently, several people heard the songs and wanted a meeting. They wanted us to meet at Derek's house.

Sebbe said, "No."

"Why not?" I stammered.

Tony was shocked, too, but waited.

Sebbe finally answered with an unenthusiastic "OK!"

We ended up taking a cab from our pathetic 4th-floor walk up to the other side of town.

Derek's girlfriend cooked a great meal; we drank the wine and passed the joints. After the first course of the meal, Derek played one of the songs. The producers, whom Derek knew, were speechless. They loved it!

For the next two hours, we ate, listened to a cut, talked, ate more, listened more, smoked more, and in the end, everyone was wowed beyond belief. We were actually offered contracts, for real, by well-known studios. Remember, they were all afraid of missing the next Beatles. But Sebbe said no to all of them. And it started again, why not? He never told anyone why, so we just called it a night and left. What a show it had been, and we were stars! Derek was quite the genius himself. I could get analytical and philosophical about how we missed that streaming meteor, but the bottom line was Sebbe wanted to become known as the greatest pop singer of all time. He already assumed the name 'The Old Man of Pop.' Our act was completed.

Later, Sebbe called Derek, "I am ready to record. My terms are that all monies earned travel through our account, and we will distribute as owed. I will decide how and when everything happens. I own all the rights and will pay those who helped handsomely, but they will not own my songs."

So there went the recording contract that had been offered. It had included a handsome promotional budget too. We never got that close again. In fact, we got arrested for possession of hashish shortly after that night.

We had moved into a house that was frequented by dealers, but it was free to rent. We were broken, and believe me, we weren't buying or selling drugs. We couldn't even afford food. We were B R O K E. It was down to begging for money on the streets to eat. Our arrest was the classic wrong place at the wrong time syndrome.

A few weeks later, I returned to the US, and I never saw Sebbe again (this seems to be a repeating theme in my life ... never seeing someone again). The night in an English prison was scary enough. The court proceedings and how my father handled everything are worth noting.

Surrounded By Heat

It was February 1968, my third session with Jack and Charlotte in London began. My return was, in a sense, a 'coming home' of sorts. There was a moment of clarity that allowed me to heal a bit. In a drug addiction state, it is all about changing everything in your life, including people the most. My new friends were very good people, some I still associate with today. I stopped all drug intake and focused on school, even finding a girl or two—ones that were positive in my life. The group these new friends started was called 'Lads and Lasses' and I was invited in. We drank at the tea house and smoked cigarettes before classes started. Cigarettes and pub crawling became my favorite pastime.

Before the beginning of my senior year, our family took a vacation to Majorca off the east coast of Spain. I would water ski, drink red wine, and lay on the beach during the day. At night we dressed in our best clothing and had great dinners in the hotel restaurant. Once everyone went to bed, I went to the local town with the band members when they were done entertaining the guests. While they spoke Spanish, I only spoke English, but we all spoke beer and fun.

By this time, my hair had grown back to a decent length, and Jack allowed it ... that's right ... allowed it. After two weeks of just plain "great," we headed back to London and off to school, work, and the merry-go-round called life. I walked into my homeroom at the American School of London (ASL) ... tan, rested, and ready ... wearing a superb brown suit with mint green pinstripes and a double-breasted jacket. My shirt was also mint green, and the tie was smartly fixed and played well with both colors. The calf-high dress boots finished off the look. I felt good for the first time in no telling how long.

As I passed through the door, I immediately spotted a girl (from Redondo Beach, California) and a boy (from New York City). I looked at them ... they looked at me ... and we all knew that we were stoners all the way. Well, that was the beginning of the end ... there are a bunch of stories that go hand in hand with these two characters ... and I am sure I will get around to some of them later ... but let's just say my old ways were on the rise ... and all of the progress and nice clothes were on their way out. I even remember trying to decide whether to go to France on the senior class ski trip or leave home in the middle of the night to live in poverty and imagination. I left home ... never to return. What was I thinking? Later on, that!

So, January 1970 rolls around and I am back in California. I am staying in Juanita's apartment while trying to reconnect with the peeps and get enrolled in a junior college ... junior college meant junior money from Jack. It did not take me long to find my old cronies ... my best of the best friends. I ended up living with a friend and his girlfriend in Laguna Beach. This house was cool, but my friend became a drug dealer. It was January 1970, and this beach town was the center of the drug universe. My friend took over and pushed the nosy neighbors back to their own world and began our lifestyle of the rich and stupid.

I came home one evening and found my friend and his girlfriend fighting ... big time, yelling and screaming and breaking things like the bathroom cabinet that was full of illegal pills that were now all over the floor. Remember, this was 1970, and illegal pills were not a traffic ticket offense yet. Needless to say, here comes the police. The neighbors finally found a way to nose back in.

Knock, knock, knock, and the man was in. He looked around and looked at my friend and his girlfriend and then saw the pills, "One of you has to go?" is all the cop said.

My friend grabbed his coat and keys, then split like a good boy. The police followed him out, and I closed and locked the door behind them.

Chris closed the curtains, and I began picking up the pills. We found all the other drugs ... theirs and mine and got everything near the toilet ... ready to flush. As we got ready for the worst, the noise outside picked up.

I went to look out the window, and the yard was filled with squad cars. We were surrounded ... trapped like rats. My decision meant abandoning ship. So, I cracked the back door and waited ... nothing happened ... I opened it wide enough to slip outside ... nothing happened ... I crept to the edge and peeped again ... they were still there, but a couple of the cars had left. My car was down the street, and no one noticed my exit. I slid quietly through the gate and rode the shadows down the street to my VW.

Whether they ever knocked or tried to enter again that night is unknown. There had been several nights prior to that where hundreds of pounds of grass were present and sold. My friend was dealing heavy ... that wasn't my thing ... but I am sure I was guilty by association. It wasn't long after that we all split up and went our own way. I never saw his girlfriend again, and he died tragically a year or two later. And I am still pissed at him for leaving me with all the great memories of our adventures and no one to share them with ... damn.

13

Search and Rescue

I was way into riding off-road at this time in my life. I think it was about 1979 or 1980. Honda had just come out with the three-wheelers. They were small bores at the time but they could climb just about everything. I had a few friends who were also into off-roading. A couple of them were always ready to go.

I am not sure how Lance knew Ronnie ... but Ronnie was rich in our terms. He drove a new truck and owned this great travel trailer. He invited us to go riding, and somehow, we ended up leaving for this pretty remote place called the Dumont Dunes. This was a set of sand dunes in the California high desert near the Nevada state line just north of Baker. When we got there, it was very hot, and we were drinking pretty heavily. We went riding anyway. Lance was a very good rider and he was riding a 390 Husky. The problem was he could only ride so far before he fell ... and he was taking some bad falls.

We finally dragged him back to camp while he was still alive.

There were some weird dudes who kept hanging around ... I asked if they bothered anyone else ... Ronnie opened a drawer and pulled out a shiny .357 Magnum pistol, smiled, and said ... not me. Lance opened a closet, pulled out a 12-gauge shotgun, and smiled ... no one will mess with us. They were full of shit, but it was nice to know we had it if we needed it. Instead of hanging around, we loaded the bikes, folded camp, and drove off, looking for the way back to the highway ... in the dark. We found the highway and a very cool trailer park where we parked, drank more, and BBQ'd some steaks. We watched Johnny Carson on the TV and smoked a few joints before passing out.

The next day we still wanted to ride, so we set off looking for another place that wasn't 115 degrees in the morning. Somehow, we ended up in Death Valley. There were tons of great dunes, but they were not accessible by truck, and I believe they were not open to off-road anyway. So, we kept drinking Greyhounds by the pitcher and driving through the desert ... until we came out on the other side ... at the base of the Sierra Mountains. After some investigation, we found a highway that led up into the mountains and took us to a place called

Kennedy Meadows. There was a great campground ... practically empty ... and off-road riding was permitted. We had a blast ... we rode for hours and finally stopped at dusk. We drank and smoked and enjoyed our newfound venue.

The next day, I started putting things away for the Sunday truck home. Ronnie and Lance ... neither were married, and neither had kids ... looked at me and said ... we're staying another day.

I said, "I couldn't ... I have to be home."

They replied, "Too bad ... we're going riding, and we'll leave tomorrow."

Now, I was sort of wild, but I knew not getting home and being off the grid with no contact—there were no phones up there—was not wild; it was rude. But what could I say or do?

So, I did not ride that day ... I hung around and smoked shitty weed that gave me a headache, and basically felt uneasy.

The next day, we finally rolled down the mountain ... it was Monday, and we stopped around 11 am for breakfast in a small desert town. I found a pay phone called home.

When Ruth answered, she was immediately relieved to hear my voice ... then she got ugly ... where

235

are you? Johannesburg, I answered ... where have you been? Kennedy Meadows, I answered ... why didn't you call? There were no phones, and Ronnie refused to drive me anywhere, but the Grumpy Bear Bar, and there were no phones there either.

She had been calling the police, who called search and rescue, who flew several times over the Dumont Dunes looking for us. We were not there. They even suggested that we might have gone to Las Vegas, which was two hours away. She said I wouldn't do that without calling ... she was right ... they laughed at her and ended the search. All in all, I felt pretty bad ... and Ronnie and Lance didn't feel a bit bad ... it was all about the adventure ... and they were right ... the difference was no one would miss them for days if they didn't come back. They pulled up to the curb in front of my house, threw me and my things on the lawn, and sped away ... you just have to watch who you roll with, you know!

Hey Danny

I was 21 years old ... a college dropout, and a printer. I worked at this shop in Orange County, California ... I was, at this time, a cutter-folder operator ... which meant I cut paper and then folded it on machines. I also did some binding too. But mostly, I would cut and fold paper in preparation for the binding process. I was actually pretty good at it, and I worked from 2 pm to 10:30 pm, which worked for me. I could sort of come and go as I pleased as long as I finished what was asked of me each night.

I had this 1957 VW that I bought from Pete, who moved back to Florida. I needed a place to live. His roommate needed another roommate, and I could have half of the house if I bought his car. Done deal. This car was cool, and it had a good radio, which drowned out the noise the three remaining cylinders made.

One night at work, there was this really hard job to fold ... it was on a plastic type of paper, and it was not easy to set up the machine to feed it and fold it. I had it running pretty well by break time, so I punched out and drove quickly to a friend's house and bought two lids of grass (I know everyone knows what a lid is, but I'll clarify anyway ... it is an ounce of grass in a sandwich baggie).

I went back to work ... punched in, and folded paper all night long. Although I usually quit at 10:30 pm, I wanted to be the hero, so I stayed until 4 am and finished the job. I felt pretty good about this accomplishment ... so I rolled a joint for the ride home.

I lived up in the canyons, so I waited until I was out of the city and on the country road to light up. I was rolling along, enjoying the tunes, when I dropped the half-smoked and lit joint onto the floorboard of my car. I felt around for a few seconds and could not find it, but I could smell it burning. I looked in my rear-view mirror ... something I did by habit and noted that there was no one in view ... so I pulled over, got out, and started feeling around in the dark for the joint. I had no idea how stoned I was or how long I looked, but I suddenly heard something behind me.

I stood up, turned around, and was face to face with an O.C. Sheriff. He asked, "What are you doing?"

My car was smoking like Spicoli's van in "Fast Times." I quickly answered, "I have engine trouble."

And he looks at me with that "really?" look and says, "... in the front seat of a VW?"

"Please step away from your car."

Then he radios in to see if I have any outstanding warrants ... which I do not. Then asks if he can look around my car while he is waiting on the warranty. *I can say no? How?*

So, I said sure ... in a couple of minutes, he returned with the two lids ... tossed them on the hood of his car, and said, "... you are under arrest ... please turn around and put your hands on the hood of the car."

After he handcuffs me and reads me my rights, he asks me why I have two individually bagged ounces of grass, and I tell him the truth ... so I only have to make this trip every two weeks. He says you are under arrest on three felony counts ... transportation, possession, and intent to sell. My heart sank ... this was the big one. But my mind was on fire, and I was actually pissed ... what the fuck ... I just worked 14 fucking hours, and I live in a shack, and I drive a piece of shit car ... what kind of dealer am I?

A fucking loser or stupid or better yet, both! So, I cannot keep my mouth shut, and I say ... when you get home tonight and pour your fucking martini remember me ... you are no different ... you are the same as me ... you just use alcohol ... I smoke pot. And you know I am not a dealer.

The ride to the county facility was quiet, and the sun was rising ... he was tired ... I was asleep most of the way ... the handcuffs were really tight, and my hands

239

were asleep too. When we pulled into the jail facility ... he stopped the car, looked over his shoulder and asked me one more time ... why the two ounces? I look him right in the eyes and tell him again ... I buy them two at a time, so I don't have to go to the dealer and drive with them every week. He gets out ... opens my door, and pulls me out. He leads me over to the booking officer and says ... book him on misdemeanor possession of marijuana. With that, he looks at me for a second and walks away. I never saw him again ... but I must have reached him somehow.

By the time I get through the booking process, it is 7 am on Friday morning, and I have one phone call before they lock me up. I dial my brother Danny ... he answers ... I quickly explain the position ... ask him to drive to my place of employment ... get my paycheck and take it to a bail bond office near the jail and get me the fuck out! He says OK, he will do that. I am put in a third-floor lock-up, which is a community holding tank that houses 100 people who have not yet been arraigned. I am given a bunk where I go to sleep and wait for Danny to spring me.

It was breakfast on the Sunday ... three days later ... that had me worried and confused. What had gone wrong ... why was I still there, and how was I going to survive much longer? I am going to blog later about the time I spent inside this jail and the court appearance because that is a long story on its own ... but for now, I will finish by telling you my roommate finally realized something was up ... called around ... found me ... drove straight there and bailed me out. I walked out at 4 pm that afternoon ... went straight to a pay phone, and dialed Danny. It rang a couple of times, and he answered ... I said ... hey Danny ... and before I could say anything else, he let out this gasp that said it all ... he was messed up when I called ... said OK ... hung up ... went back to sleep, and three and a half days later, only remembered when he heard my voice. Shit happens.

More "Hey Danny" Adventure

I need to finish this story ... there is more to tell for sure. Remember that I had just been bailed out of jail by my roommate, who noticed my dog came home, and I didn't ... he found me in jail on a Sunday afternoon and bailed me out immediately.

As I was being booked into the O.C. jail facility, I thought about the previous couple of hours I had spent in the custody of the arresting officer. He was going to have me booked on three felonies, which, if I was convicted, could have landed me in jail for at least a year and very probably longer. It was 1972 ... I had long hair, and the laws regarding drug possession and use were much harder than they are now. He had decided I was telling the truth ... which I was ... and had made a monumental decision in my favor and had me booked on a low-level charge. He could have had me booked on driving under the influence of drugs with felony reckless driving added on. That would have been jail time, too ... but he didn't, and that could have changed my life dramatically ... I am only guessing on that thought.

Even my redneck neighbor from next door chimed in on this event. He was an OK guy with a strange way of being neighborly. When I first moved in, he came over and said we could do whatever we wanted ... as long as we did it on our own property ... he would be cool. The morning I was being arrested, he drove by on his way to work ... he stopped over later to tell me I should cut my hair ... if I would, they would leave me alone. As strange as that sounded, it turned out that he was basically right.

These three days in jail had impacted me. I was locked up with 99 other guys ... and some of them were hardcore. One guy had his cigarettes stolen and searched everyone's area looking for them ... muttering something about cutting whoever had them. I knew I hadn't taken them but that didn't mean someone else hadn't and put them with my belongings. As it turned out, he never found them, and no one got cut. Some guy in one of the two-man cells on the second floor cut himself in a suicide attempt ... lots of screaming and blood. Our holding tank was a revolving door ... someone was always going home, and someone was always coming in. The food was scary, and I didn't eat it until the end of the second day. Hunger won that battle. In the end, I made a life decision ... I was not going to last inside of a jail system ... I needed to make this my last stay.

My arraignment was held on election day in 1972 ... and guess what ... legalizing marijuana was on the ballot ... that's right ... the first-ever attempt to spit in J. Edgar Hoover's beer was on the ballot ... the very day I was being prosecuted for possession ... I was incensed. I got to court early and found the DA ... I was pissed and wanted to talk to him ... he was amused and asked me what I wanted ... I told him to either put me in jail and pay my rent or send me back to work ... but do it today ... I was not going to hire an attorney ... I was not playing the game anymore (what was I thinking?). He literally told me to calm down ... then he read the report and my rap sheet and decided that since I had spent three days in jail ... paid to have my car towed, and posted bail ... this was enough punishment for his liking ... he offered me a $100 fine and two years informal probation. I was stunned at how easy that had been ... a good deal and all I had to do was snivel. I guess he had kids too.

Then I asked him what would happen if the pot initiative passed on the ballot today ... he didn't know, so he asked the judge when my case was called ... the judge said he would throw the case out ... I asked for a one-day extension and got it. The initiative failed ... I returned to court the next day ... and another (younger)

DA had gotten hold of my case and denied the settlement ... asking for more jail time because of my prior arrests. I blew up and found the older guy from the day before and asked him what the fuck? He tried to reason with the young guy and finally came back and said ... keep the $100 and do one more weekend in the county; that's the best I can do today. Fuck ... back to jail ... and the scary part was not the people or the time ... it was the trouble that could happen and the possibility of not getting back out on Sunday.

I rose and listened while the judge spoke ... he said, "... Thomas ... you have a very interesting rap sheet ... you have been in trouble several times since 1967 ... you have escaped every time with the minimum of consequences ... it appears you are a liar too. Any of this does not fool me ... so I am going to write on your permanent record that I am recommending one-year minimum in the county jail if you are convicted of anything else ... plea bargain or not ... even jaywalking ... do I make myself clear?" I was stunned ... this meant there were no more chances ... I swallowed hard and said,"... yes ... I understand." And even though I understood ... I was unable to stop taking the chances ... and it wasn't until June of 1984, when I got sober, that I stopped looking in the rear-view mirror ... in my car and in my life.

As I write this tonight ... 39 years later ... 27 clean and sober ... I remember how many times I tempted fate with my actions. Although I survived that last weekend in jail, it was only luck or Divine intervention that kept me out of harm's way between November of 1972 and June of 1984 when I got clean and sober. And you know ... I feel serendipity played a part, too ... I did meet the right people, and I did change my life as a result. My dad (Jack) told me that I was going to end up digging a ditch for a living ... that was a bad thing to him ... but he asked me to please dig the best ditch I knew how if that ended up happening. I do have blisters from my professional life, and I have dug the best ditch I know how to.

Love It or Leave It

I think the year was 1970 ... either way ... wherever I was living did not afford me the opportunity to wash my clothes. Juanita lived nearby, and I would often go there to use her facility to have something to eat and watch some TV.

One night, I was hanging around waiting on the dryer. Juanita was out drinking somewhere ... I think with a girlfriend ... but I cannot really remember who was in this story ... except Juanita, me, and someone she picked up and brought home. Now remember ... this was her home and her life. I am not being judgmental ... I may say some off-the-wall things about her, but she was my mother and had a great heart. OK ... her thinking was a bit screwed up, and I would say that my screwy thinking came to me naturally ... while living out the Juanita odyssey.

I am doing whatever I do when the door opens, and they come in ... I think there may have been two guys, Juanita and her girlfriend. They were loud, and they had been drinking ... I guess they were drunk ... whatever that means. The apartment was a cheap stucco and drywall place that was one of many that circled a cheap pool. Almost nothing that was said above an average voice level could go unheard by the neighbors. Like I said, they were loud this evening, and I was worried about the neighbors ... the neighbors!

I was 20 years old ... I was thin and had long hair pulled back in a ponytail. I was wearing bell-bottom striped pants and a T-shirt ... that is as much as I remember about me that evening. It was 1970 ... just three years after the summer of love ... anti-war rallies were literally everywhere on the globe ... the whole world wanted the US out of Vietnam. I am not educated in history, but I am sure that money ... and a lot of it ... was at the root of this war. I had just returned from London, where 500,000 Europeans had marched on the US Embassy in Grosvenor Square. Everyone knew this war was a bad scene, and no one knew how to stop it.

What this history lesson on Vietnam does for you tonight is to help you understand what took place at Juanita's. I can describe this one guy ... the one I remember ... not by sight recognition ... but by memory of his essence. I can describe him because "they" were all the same. He would have been wearing a sports shirt and jacket ... his pants would have been pleated ... his belly would have hung over his belt, and his shoes would have needed a good shine to be decent again. The alcohol in his system would have made his tongue loose.

As Juanita and whoever else was there were pouring drinks in the kitchen this guy slid up close to me and asked why I wear my hair so long. OH no. I tell him because that is how I like to wear it. He takes a quantum leap right into my face as he leans over and says ... if you don't love this country, why don't you leave it? OK ... he's drunk ... I'm cramping his style because I'm there, and he's hoping to get lucky and get home before his wife and kids miss him. But something happened deep inside of me at that very moment. After years of being afraid of these guys in my world ... the ones who gave me money to go play outside ... the ones who locked me out of my own home so I wouldn't interrupt their sexual exploitation of Juanita ... the ones I hated to the bottom of my soul ... I snapped.

I watched the cocky son of a drunken bitch coast back into the kitchen and sit down at my mother's table. He looked at me as if to say ... get fucking lost, you loser. I rose and walked over to him and said as calmly as I could under the circumstances ... if I ever have children, they will be a thousand times the man you arc, you fucking jerk ... now stand up. He said ... why? I said because I am going to put your fucking head right through that fuckin' wall, and I will do it while you are sitting if you prefer ... but I am going to fucking mess you up, you piece of shit (is an exclamation mark necessary here?).

I had hit his nerve right on the head ... he sprung from his chair ... his friend (yep, I just remembered for sure ... he had a friend with him) raced to grab him ... Juanita began slapping me and yelling at me to shut up as I let loose with a barge of four-letter words, leaving nothing; I was feeling uncovered. I really hated this guy ... so much so that my fear had fled, and I was set free. But he was subdued by his friend, and I was over my physical indignation, and Juanita was stunned ... and get this ... embarrassed by my behavior. I was done. I took my wet clothes from the dryer and walked out the door.

I never spoke to my mother about that night ... I just didn't care. I never washed my clothes there again, and I never dealt with her behavior and the men she hung out with again, either. Even though I have not lived at home since March of my senior year in high school, this night was surely the moment I knew I would never call Juanita's my home again.

Learning How to Talk ... Again

Life at the American School in London was rolling along, but I was way out of bounds again. Although I had enjoyed a clean semester and a summer before I stumbled again. I had forgotten where I came from and settled into the life of a promising young man living in a foreign country. I was losing my grip. I had returned from a great vacation in the Mediterranean with the family ... tan, rested and ready. I walked into my homeroom, and there were Annie and Ronnie ... two peas from the same pod I had come from. I have already spoken about Ronnie and his ability to get prescriptions for uppers and downers ... and I did love downers ... damn, I was weak ... in fact ... if I had to pinpoint the last chance, I had to pull out of the Odyssey it was at that moment in my life ... I hit the wall instead.

I did what I did best ... I turned off the feelings and excelled in the fine art of deception. I ran with them, and I slept with Annie, and I spent nights out, and I infuriated my father, and I stressed out what had almost been a good thing for him and me ... and I broke it for good. And all of that because I needed something that people like Ronnie and Annie never had and could never have and share ... I was the problem though ... so I just kept rolling in lieu of knowing what else to do.

There was this French chic named Nellie ... I do not know where she came from ... whose friend she was, or even where she lived ... but I knew we were going to spend some time together. And there was this other girl named Holly ... she was not striking or hip or cool, but she was very nice, and I think, looking back, she was probably a very interesting person given the chance. And she had a crush on me ... proof positive she was a needy individual. So, she arranges to throw a parent approved party at her London home. The entire downstairs was for us ... we could drink and dance and crash there and everything was good. And best of all, Nellie was going to be there too. I took 2 or 3 reds (again ... reds are a barbiturate ... a sleeping pill made by the drug company Lilly). I could take them by the handful back in the States, and 2 or 3 sounded right. What I had not factored in was my clean system ... danger, danger, danger.

Let's cut to the chase ... shortly after the party started to roll, I started to drink a little, and the pills started to kick in, and before I knew it, I was beginning to spin. Nellie and I were starting to get close just before I fell off the face of the earth ... everyone was standing there watching as I began to spin. I had been in similar

252

spots before, and I instinctively knew that I had to hang on until this state of intoxication subsided. I ended up in the bathroom ... I was muy sick, and I had long since stopped thinking about Nellie ... and believe me when I tell you that later, I was really depressed about missing that opportunity ... and it never presented itself again either. But Holly was very cool ... I can remember her talking to me and encouraging me not to pass out ... and she would say ... I've got to get my parents ... and I would answer ... no no, no, I can handle this, I will be OK.

After a while, I stopped having a memory ... but I did hang in there, and by the time the sun came up, I was beginning to have coherent thoughts. I was so fucked up I do not even remember who was still there ... or what anyone said to me ... and worst of all, I have no recollection of Holly that morning. It was all about me ... typical of my self-centered thinking. Here was a very cool girl who had helped me survive while I was destroying her party and probably scaring her to death. I had such little respect for myself that I never even contemplated the fact that I nearly died of a drug overdose ... how could I have had any concern for anyone else? This was another aha moment ... who was I, and what was happening to me?

And here's the kicker: I was skiing in Switzerland for two weeks over the Christmas Holiday. Jack had not given up on me ... or maybe he just wanted me out of his house for a few days ... sort of like Juanita sending me to his place for the summers ... a little downtime. But I had to meet him at Harrods in the West End to buy ski boots that morning. After I had washed up the best I could, I left Holly's to find a bus ... and once out in the world, I noticed my motor skills were super impaired ... in fact, I could barely talk while asking for a ticket on the bus. I was freaked out ... the overdose had dented me pretty well, and I was afraid Jack would pick up when he saw me and listened to my slurred words. I had a plan ... I always had a plan ... they often worked but were always sad thinking.

I arrived at Harrods a few minutes before our scheduled rendezvous and, went to several departments and asked questions about different items. I was practicing talking ... the more I talked, the better it got, and after a few minutes of interaction, my motor skills started to stabilize. When I met up with Jack, he appeared to be none the wiser ... and if he noticed my tilted walk, he did not say a word about it ... he was either hung over himself ... highly likely ... or not willing to attempt to stem the tide of my demise anymore.

We bought ski boots and made it home. He drove, and I watched the world roll by. I made it to school on Monday, and as expected, no one said a word ... at least not to me ... about the party. There is no doubt that many of these kids had never seen someone nearly die ... and if I wasn't scared by what happened, I am sure some of them were. I really only remember two things ... I let Holly down ... she never talked to me again, and I missed my chance with Nellie ... beyond that, learning to talk again was the highlight of the weekend.

14

SOOAD Plain's

The bizarre adventure of my life continued in 1969. I had left home and yet somehow finished high school. We lived off Baker Street in West London. At the time, my roommates were Sebbe, the writer, and Dihilo, his girlfriend. Another couple shared the space and lived in the master bedroom. Plus, the space case who lived in the front bedroom. We all shared the rest of the house. The others in the house slept at night and worked and went to school during the days, but Sebbie and I slept during the day and roamed the city at night.

Once, we bought animated sculptures, brought home milk bottles and beer bottles, and created a four-foot chessboard. We had to climb up on furniture to get an aerial view. The others constantly complained that we kept them up and burned too much fuel to heat the house. Once, the guy from the master room came shivering at four in the morning ... when he opened the door, the hot air rushed out and nearly burned his eyebrows. We were deep into a game of chess and ignored him completely. The space case moved, so we took his room too. Since his move left us with more space, we bought two old upright pianos and had them professionally moved into the new space. We then started making music called, 'basic insanity.' It was rhythmic pounding on the keys of both pianos in random order. It was really great ... it vibrated the flat, and it pissed off the whole building.

One morning, when we returned from wandering the streets we found an eviction notice that our roommate had stuck to the front door with this huge kitchen knife ... it was priceless ... we didn't care ... we'd move. But once inside the house, Sebbe pretended to pull a knife on me ... so I pretended to pull a knife on him, and we began to circle each other, looking for an opportunity to lunge for the kill. In no time, we were wildly out of control, fighting for our lives ... pushing, kicking ... rolling over furniture ... it was an all-out brawl.

Dihilo took cover, screaming the whole time. I know this sounds untrue, but we were both into 'not dying' at the hands of the other. Eventually, I was killed, and we collapsed in exhaustion. I am guessing the entire event took five minutes ... but it sparked a thought ...

what if ... what if we hunted each other in the park in the middle of the night?

The next night, we entered Regents Park after midnight. Our rules included pretending to be riding horses ... gallop away, and then do your best to circle back under cover and shoot your adversary. Yep ... we were playing guns with nothing but our imagination ... in the dead of night ... in a huge park that was closed. It was our high plains, and we hunted for a long time, for many nights, and we perfected the rules. It almost seemed real.

I still remember being alone in a dark wooded area ... fearing Sebbe's fake gunshot more than the weirdos who haunted parks at night. Oh yeah ... in this case, I guess we were the weirdos.

Our goal was to make a ton of money in the music business ... buy a ton of land in the US Midwest and, build separate homes, and hunt each other with BB guns ... that's right ... BB guns with leather clothing and eye protection ... that was our goal in 1969. Sebbe even came up with a name for this place ... SOOAD Plains ... which stood for Straight Out of a Dream. We even had a song titled "SOOAD Plains." ... I think I can still strum it on the guitar.

Well, you know we never achieved SOOAD Plains or many of the crazy things we dreamed of ... but we did have a very good time. London at night was our playground ... we even played soccer in the underground tunnels of the parks used by the maintenance crews during the day. We smoked joints in front of the Marriott Hotel on Park Avenue and freaked out the tourists. We ate at really nice restaurants, dressed in 3-piece suits, tennis shoes, and strings of pearls draped around our wrists and necks. We'd get accosted by English Bobbies in Piccadilly Circus at three in the morning and then walk for miles across all the parks in the city. But always after they were closed. We dealt with the weird ones and the Bobbies on bicycles. We loved the city after dark. In a way, it was SOOAD Plains!

Head On ... My Friend #1

Anyone alive has been faced with someone they loved or know developing cancer and passing away. In 1999, a very good friend's wife faced lung cancer. So, she called me and asked me to go with Monty to the superbike races in Laguna Seca, just outside Monterrey. She needed him to get away for a spell. I had gone once before and gladly went again.

After we agreed to go, Monty called, "The hotels are booked; we will have to camp on the track."

"Even better, bike camping!"

At the time, I had a customized Honda 1100 cc Spirit. It was completely decked out with lots of power. Monty had a 1200 cc BMW road bike. We met early on Friday morning and circled LA, slid through the foothills, and over to the coast along Ventura. Our ride up the coast was great, and we stopped for lunch in Big Sur. By the time we arrived, the place was filling up, so we found a place to camp quickly. It was along the race track on Ridge Road near the corkscrew turn. We made camp, got some food, and settled in for the night.

It was quite a night ... the Euro bikers were out in force, the entire road bike world seemed to be camped there. I had no idea there were so many avid riders who didn't dress like the Hell's Angels. As the night wore on ... and I was told there were 50,000 camped out. I think that was overstated, but there were a bunch, that's for sure ... it got crazier and crazier.

Monty and I didn't drink or smoke dope ... we were clean and sober (Monty died that way, and I am still that way), but we stayed up and watched the insanity of fireworks, drunks, and cops ... it was quite the happening. We stayed until Sunday and then split ... Monty left for Bend, Oregon, and I left for Southern Cal. We had a great time and rode away separately. We rolled independently ... it was a good fit for sure.

In 2001, after Carol passed away, Monty and I decided to go back to the races. The loss really affected him, and he lost his long-time dog. But we rallied and met for an early coffee and struck out on another adventure. The ride was another good one; he was on the same BMW I had transferred to an 1800 cc Yamaha Road Star—also painted and customized. It was a great bike, maybe my favorite of all times. We reached the track, camped out, and enjoyed the show and the races. On Sunday, we left together and stopped in Santa Cruz to visit his son, whom I had never met but recently had been paroled from prison. I never asked about his crime, but I don't think he and Monty had much going on between them.

We left Santa Cruz and headed over Highway 152. We were going to cross the foothills, pick up the 5 Hwy, and cruise home together on a 90-degree 4th of July summer night. The ride was beautiful ... for a while. I was sailing through the twists and turns with ease and thinking about nothing really when I noticed something to my left. In the blink of an eye, I saw a car bank off the mountainside, coming out of a turn and veering across the center line, heading right at me. I was braking hard without going down, leaning left for all I was worth. Just as I thought to be in the clear, he turned abruptly right to avoid going off the edge ... we hit nearly head-on. Time got really slow; I rose up out of the saddle ... cleared the handlebars ... and gained altitude as I rotated head over heels in midair. I remember seeing the tree tops and my boots in the same frame ... that was not a good sight. The acknowledgment of seeing the accident take place is unimaginable. Upon impact, I expected to go blank.

I hit fairly flat but didn't roll off the side. However, I was able to land without hitting my head. Although, the landing left me loopy for a while. Then I felt my hip and leg twitch, and I chose not to look. But my bike was another story. It was fully smashed, stuck to the 1989 Lincoln. The driver was nodding a little when I went off with a barrage of four-letter words. Needless to say, I was fucking pissed ... my bike was toast ... my ride was done ... my weekend was done ... all I wanted to do was scream ... and that is what I did.

Stay tuned ... I will finish this!

Head On ... My Friend #2

The rage came to a head; I wanted to rip the drunk fuckers face off his body. Then suddenly ... after I stopped screaming, this very nice lady ... whose name or face I cannot remember kneels down to hold my hand.

She told me, "We had been trying to call the highway patrol for 10 minutes. We were right behind him, and he was all over the road. I am a nurse ... what is your name, and how do you feel?"

I began to calm down and realized there was nothing to be done and how lucky I was to just be alive. She helped me move to the side of the road and placed my head on the asphalt curbing. I was lying flat and comfortable. At that moment, the drunk opened his door, stepped out of his car ... and right off the edge of the road and down the hillside. The crowd went running, screaming at the man. It took a few minutes to get him back up the hillside and seated down next to me.

Monty was in the lead, had seen the drunk and knew something was wrong. He turned back and found me on the ground. When he saw the drunk driver, he jumped off his bike. He took one look at us and stopped screaming. The drunk was bloody from head to toe. I was just scraped up a bit with a couple of fractured bones.

Monty looked at the drunk, "I'm gonna kick your fucking head in! Should I do it?"

He looked at me, and I said, "No, that won't help."

The nurse patted my hand and said, "Now, Monty, this is all about Tom, and he doesn't need that."

"Should I?"

He looked at me again, and I said, "No."

"What should I do then?" He asked.

"I think you should just get on your bike and go home. There is nothing you can do. I'll be fine when I get to the hospital. I will just catch a flight home and might even beat you there. :)"

"Fine ..." he said and left. That's the way we roll.

When the highway patrol arrived, they thought the drunk had been riding the bike. He was torn up badly. They finally figured out he had been driving the car. Then the cops asked him what happened.

The drunk said, "He came across the road and hit me head-on."

The cop looked at the skid marks and asked him, "Have you been drinking?"

"I had a few beers," he said. Classic response. He went to jail.

I heard the cop say they called this road Blood Alley. I said, "You know if I knew they called this road blood alley, I would have taken a different route."

The only other thing I remember was the ambulance came to give me a ride, and the nurse was ready to start an IV in my arm. I objected.

The driver got pissed and said, "Whatever, dumb bikers. Just let him die."

I said, "Fine, go ahead." But right then, we stopped at a landing zone.

"The chopper is here; let them deal with him," said the driver

The ambulance left, and the chopper loaded me through the cylindrical tail section. I am claustrophobic and started to panic.

I looked up, and two paramedics were leaning over, "You are going to be okay."

They put the IV in and started asking questions. In a few minutes, the ship starts shaking fiercely, and I think ... great ... now I am going to die in a chopper. They said not to worry; it always shakes on the landing. Then they pull me out the same way, on a rolling table, heading directly to the operating room. I remember the doctor appeared to be a Prince look alike.

They cut my clothes off. Now I am broken, freaked out, and naked.

"What hurts?" They asked.

"My hip a little."

"Where's the helmet?" Yelled the doctor.

The ER staff handed him a 'novelty plastic lid', "Is this your helmet?"

He said, "Yeah, that looks just like it."

"This is a piece of shit! While you are here, go to the 5th floor and see all of the quadriplegics who landed on their heads."

"No thanks," I replied.

They sent me to Admitting for a thorough inspection. On the way down, I saw the nurse and said, "You cut off my clothes; you ruined them. Now you need to find me pants and a T-shirt so I can fly home."

"I will she said."

When I got Admitting, they asked, "Do you have contacts?"

"No, I am an orphan; I have no relatives," I said.

They don't believe me, but I insist ... I didn't want them calling anyone. "I am ready to be released. And I need a cab to the airport."

The other nurse returned with some funky clothes, but they worked. The woman in admitting called

267

the on-duty doctor who looked at my clipboard, "You aren't going anywhere, you are on a 24-hour hold, and we need to take an MRI of your hip ... if it is broken, you may be bleeding internally."

Great ... just what I need. So, I turned to admitting, "I need a phone."

They said, "I thought you were an orphan."

I stayed almost two days, but the soreness settled in fast. They tried to insist, "No, I'm a recovery addict."

He made me sit up straight, "As long as you lay flat and don't move, you'll be fine."

But then he started to push on my back; the pain was excruciating. "If you intend to ride in a car heading home, you need to be able to get out of bed."

So, I spent the night on a morphine drip and, in the morning, started the Vicodin. I cried all the way to the car that afternoon. Stay tuned ... there is #3, but I want to talk about my family, my recovery, and my next bike ... yep, I bought another one. However, my twelve-year-old daughter cried.

"You need to stop; I'm not going to die on a bike."

Head On … My Friend #3

Needless to say, the hospital in San Jose stunk. My wife and twelve-year-old daughter drove all night to greet me in the morning. I wanted to get the hell out of there, but the nurses would not feed me. Finally, I'd had enough and demanded to see a doctor.

He arrived within minutes. "What's going on, why won't you feed me?"

"We were not feeding you, not knowing if you needed surgery yet."

"If I need surgery, no one here is getting the job. I have a bone doctor at home, and trust him."

He smiled, "Okay, then remove the IV and feed him."

It was at this time that I learned that I needed the pain meds. I ended up staying another night the next day. After we finally got out, it was time to get in the Dodge Durango. Boy, did that suck! Talk about white with pain. On the way home, we made a pit stop at the tow yard to see about my bike. They went back and took a picture, then pulled my personal stuff off. It was the last time I saw my bike. My wife and daughter were cool. I really appreciated the way they cared.

The next day, nodding off on Vicodin in a wheelchair that the hospital sold me, I got rolled to the bone doctor, who does the X-rays and exam. "Ummm, you have a cracked pelvis, collarbone, and scapula. I am recommending physical therapy. You can go home.

So, when I got home, I called the owner of the gym. He called the local chiropractor ... upstairs. "I can't help you either, but I can turn you over to a massage therapist."

The idea sounded great ... and that is where I met my healer ... Ruthie. Her approach to medicine was unlike anyone I'd ever met. The approach included burning sage. I spent two hours, three or four nights every week, while she worked on me. She was not cruel, but not a feel-good massage person either, unless she wanted to be. What she did was a deep tissue massage. It felt good to know someone located and fixed the underlying problems. Like my legs that were black and blue from hitting the handlebars ... she literally healed me.

Four months later, I was back on my dirt bike in the desert. Although the wheelchair lasted a week, the crutches lasted a month, and the walking cane lasted a month. I only missed five days of work. You have to marvel at the baby boomers ... we regularly work 60–70-

270

hour weeks without even questioning it ... and vacations are nothing more than long weekends. And oh yes ... we can get hit head-on by an '89 Lincoln and make it back to work in five days ... really something else, hey!

However, the insurance person hassled me while I was still in the wheelchair and half out of my mind on pain meds. The settlement was unacceptable. They offered $6,000 for a motorcycle in which I had invested $20,000. I had the receipts to prove it. Finally, after the arguing,

I asked for a $1,000 check. "Why, only $1,000?" They asked.

"So, I can endorse it, hand it off to my attorney, and let him figure it out."

They nodded and said they would be back the next day. The next day, they handed me a $19,000 check. :)

But wait ... there's more ... three months later she walked into my office with an envelope. "This money does not stop your medical benefits if you need them, nor will you relinquish your rights to sue ... should you decide to sue your own insurer."

The drunk driver was uninsured and had no license, but I did not sue ... not my style. So, I opened the envelope and placed a State Farm Insurance check on my desk.

We both stared at the $100,000 tax-free dollars. Would I do this again for another $100,000? No way ... but I did up my uninsured motorist insurance to $250,000 ... just in case.

15

Shortly after we survived a harrowing flight back from Isla Magdalena in Southern Baja in a 6-seat Piper (earlier story titled 'Bad Flight'), our friend Mel bought the same plane.

His rationale ... first, he could afford it, and second ... it was a sweet way to go surfing.

I really never gave it a second thought until he called, "Do you want to go to Scorpion Bay?"

This destination was about two-thirds of the way to Cabo on the Pacific side of the Baja. I did not hesitate, "Yes, I'd like to go!"

I worked until noon and met Mel at John Wayne Airport in Newport Beach. Once I found the hanger, it was time to lose the business garb. We threw in the duffle bags, helped Mel load the cooler, tent, and other survival things like sleeping bags, wetsuits, towels, and sunglasses, and then boarded the plane.

We hopped in the six-seat Piper Saratoga low wing and taxied out onto the warm-up pad. But it suddenly got awkward. Mel was reviewing a book and

273

checking things ... I was concerned ... did he need a book?

He said, "SOP and not to worry."

Pretty soon, we got the nod from the tower, "81 Yankee, you are cleared for takeoff."

In seconds we were hauling ass down the runway, climbed up quickly, and banked south towards the border.

Mel casually said, "Start watching."

"Watch for what," I asked.

"Other planes," he says. "We are flying on VFR ... visual flight rules ... look out for other flying objects."

Shit, that got my attention!!!

Mel seemed to be very cool and appeared to have everything in order ... I quickly learned the topo map and was dialed in as his navigator. I saw mountains ahead that were 3,000 feet and recommended 6,000 feet. :) In about forty-five minutes, we began to circle down. We were so high he had to bleed off altitude to land in Calexico. Then, he checked out with US customs and scheduled his return so they could meet us and search the aircraft ... SOP.

We left and immediately landed in Mexicali to check in with Mexican customs to announce our intentions. All they did was get a stamp on my passport.

Mel was in charge, and I was only the navigator. He made all of the arrangements.

We left and set the GPS for a small fishing village on the Sea of Cortez where we were going to spend the night. The plan was to make this stop by nightfall, top off the fuel, and leave early the next day for Scorpion Bay. A lot happened on the way down ... everything was new to me. At one point, while dozing, I woke from a dream that the engine had stopped. Needless to say, it startled me ... everything was fine, and we made our third landing of the day.

Of course, the final landing had to be a doozy. We dropped down right over the desert floor and lined up with a tiny dirt runway that was just beyond a rather large gully., But Mel dropped the plane spot on. Although, there was a large bump in the runway just beyond where we touched down, and the plane went airborne again. I started pushing on the floorboard like it was a brake!

Mel put it back down and stopped with plenty of room to spare. We had a good night ... ate cheap lobster ... went for a swim in the warm ocean, and turned in early.

The next morning, we were out of there quickly and headed for Scorpion Bay. As we approached the point, we could see what was called the runway thirty minutes later; it was not more than a slightly wide road cut in the middle of the desert. But we also saw some great waves and a few people in the lineup ... it was getting exciting.

Mel said, "We're going to buzz the runway and check it out before we attempt to land."

I agreed. So, we extended out over the bay ... banked left, and lined up with the runway. Mel said nothing but put the flaps down, and we flew straight in and landed. Only this time, we were a few feet off center; this was a frightening sight.

Mel moved the plane to the center half a second after touching down and glanced my way, "All good." He laughed.

Seconds later, he gently swerved while braking to avoid a large rock ... yep, rock ... that was smack in the middle of the strip.

So, we taxied over, parked next to another plane, and shut it down. I exhaled, and we both laughed ... what a trip.

Four landings in 24 hours ... two on soft, rocky dirt, and here we were at one of the premier surf spots on the west coast.

Immediately, a local pulled up in an old truck and yelled, "Vamoose a puente y surfeit grand oles?" ... or something like that.

Either way, he piled all of our gear into his truck and, for $5, took us to the point where everyone stayed. Mel was right ... what a sweet way to go surf camping ... in an airplane.

The local guy with the truck was talking about our new Coleman cooler and how nice it would be on his fishing boat. We always shared with the locals when in Mexico, and whether they had money or not, there wasn't a Big 5 Sporting Goods store anywhere to buy a cooler. So, we asked him to return in two days and take us to the plane so he could have the cooler. He was stoked, and so were we.

81 Yankee Heading Home

It was a toss-up on what was better, Scorpion Bay or the flying adventure. Mel had handled everything with confidence and skill. I was fairly relaxed for the navigation assistance on the homeward flight.

What I was not prepared for were the other people who owned the other plane. A man who was at that time a professional commercial airline pilot with thousands of hours logged in flight, his wife, and his daughter wanted us to fly home with them. He convinced Mel the flight up the Pacific coast would save us a few hours.

Mel mentioned, "We flew the Sea of Cortez coast to avoid the fog. I'm not instrument-rated."

The other pilot said, "Not to worry, you can follow me up the coast; everything will be fine."

I still don't know why he wanted or needed us to go with him. But for some reason, Mel said sure ... we're in.

The plan was to fly to a coastal destination so the other pilot could get fuel (we were topped off and ready to roll). Mel checked his book and pointed out that there was no fuel service there on Sundays.

"It's fine. I always get fuel there." We left together.

Following someone in a plane is not like following a car. As soon as we were airborne, we were in radio contact only with no visuals. Soon, we were above the cloud layer, and I wondered how this was going to play out ... but I said nothing (I think!).

Eventually, the other pilot gave Mel coordinates and instructed us to descend through the clouds, then watch for the runway as soon as we popped out. It was a tense few minutes as we flew completely blind in the clouds. When we popped out suddenly, our elevation was really low, maybe a couple of thousand feet ... I'm not sure. But finding the runway was a struggle, and we needed to find it quickly. Mel spotted it and landed ... at least it was asphalt.

Mel was right ... there was no fuel service on Sundays. The other pilot was pissed, "Well, just go on back to your original route. I'll wait and get a hotel."

Mel said, "We have enough fuel to share. So, we can transfer from ours to yours. We can backtrack to the place we stayed the first night and get fuel."

And that is what we did: drained one gallon at a time into a plastic milk carton and poured it into his plane. It took about an hour, but we got him enough to head the other way.

And once again, we followed him off the runway, through the clouds, and southeast to the other side of the peninsula.

But before long, Mel and I noticed what appeared to be a storm on its way north—we were flying straight at it. Timing is everything. We made the destination, pulled up to the fuel pump, topped both planes off, and decided to high-tail it out of there. The rain was close.

Now we were back on the east coast of Baja and following the other guy again ... still by radio only.

He yells out, "Let's take pictures of each other."

Mel said, "Okay, where are you?"

He gives us his altitude and relative location. Mel checks his GPS, "This is exactly where we are."

After a moment of silence, "You are just above me; either way, that is not good, or one of us is incorrect. Are you over land?"

"No. I am a mile offshore." Radio silence again.

Then he says, "Wait, I can see you. One should not fly over water if it can be helped. I'll guide you. Slow down and get over the beach. Hold your altitude, and I'll do the rest."

In a couple of minutes, he was flying right off our wing, and his wife and I were snapping pictures like crazy.

After that, we settled in for the tandem trip back to Browns Field just east of San Diego, where we were to land and clear customs. It was a routine flight ...

The other guy gets out of the plane, "I'm in a hurry, so let me check in first." It took thirty minutes to clear. "Thanks ..." He gets back in the plane and leaves.

By the time we finished, it was late, and we were losing daylight. All I could think of was what an asshole.

He took us off course ... took our fuel ... snaked our spot at customs, and then left us to make Mel's first-ever night landing at a very busy airport in Orange County ... on VFR.

I am here tonight, so you know Mel iced the landing, and we had a good laugh.

The trip was burned into my memory forever. I never made another trip with Mel.

I asked him how many solo hours he had under his belt when we left ... and I cannot remember exactly, but I am sure it was in the 15-hour neighborhood. Are you kidding ... 15 fucking hours. I'd trust him again; great job!

A while later, in a casual conversation with a client, I told them about the experience.

He replied, "I am a retired Navy Pilot; next time you see your friend, punch him in the nose for me."

Borrego Springs Or Mars ... You Make the Call!

In '75, I started spending time in the low desert of southern California. Many things happened in the desert, but let's talk about my feelings about things in the area. In essence, the desert became my escape hatch from a marriage that was going bad.

My goal was to create an outing spot to invite mutual friends for a couple's retreat. Nevertheless, many of our plans never see fruition. It is important to know that most ... not all ... but 2 or 3 of these trips were before the great "sober divide" that has so thoroughly defined my life.

The low desert probably occupies several hundred square miles ... but for me you can narrow that to about 100 miles. Somehow, I ended up going to hell in a handbasket in this little place called Ocotillo Wells ... just south of the Julian Mountains and just north of the Salton Sea. This was ... is ... a wasteland ... left to the coyotes, snakes, and an abundance of drunks in and on off-road vehicles. The first time I set foot in the place, I knew it was the perfect destination.

There were many trips that didn't include the family and concentrated on getting blasted and roaming the desert floor during the long, hot summer nights. And there were plenty of others who felt the same affinity with this place.

In the early days, it was unregulated, and the off-road enthusiasts were a relatively small group of people. We understood each other ... cleaned the desert floor on Sundays before heading home. We drank in small bars ... we raged in vehicles ... we camped in tents and small trailers ... we worked on engines ... we took long trips to nowhere that had interesting names ... we helped each other when things went wrong ... we raved ... we got lost and spent whole nights parked and waiting for the sun so we could find our way home while we still had gas. We shot guns and had wild sex on the top of sand dunes ... we drank wine in shot glasses at the cafe while making meaningless toasts to whatever.

Once, I was actually asked to leave the cafe because the owners liked me and couldn't bear to see me so out of it. And such was the decade of decadence drowned in gasoline, alcohol, and drugs.

But for those who survived, there was a moment of clarity that showed on us, and we simply stopped ... there was no other alternative. As for me ... I sold all the toys and trailers and got sober. Yes ... I tried to go down there in early sobriety ... but the blenders in the trailer park woke me early ... all churning out exotic drinks for breakfast ... the kinds I could no longer enjoy without remorse.

But ten years later, I made a trip back, and things were different. I had a great time and didn't need to drink or do drugs to enjoy the desert. So, I did the only logical thing: I bought a new trailer ... one that could withstand the desert weather without leaking water and sand. I put it on a full hook-up spot in the sand, built a great deck, and bought an enclosed race trailer. At that point, I bought a fabulous sand rail.

I bought a quad for my daughter ... a motorcycle for me, and one for my son ... it was heaven ... except my kids rarely came ... my wife never came, and soon it was once again my escape ... sober yes ... but an escape nonetheless.

One day, I decided to drive seventeen miles northeast to the little town of Borrego Springs and see if I could find an AA meeting. I did ... it was at the Catholic Church at 7 pm every Saturday night. This was the beginning of a shift ... for twenty-five years, I had been seventeen miles from home and never knew it. I soon made friends in Borrego and eventually bought a five-acre parcel and intended to build a round home, then retire. Here is where Mars enters the story. Yes, I am a

UFO believer! I am not sure how everyone isn't, but that's a story for another day.

So, I am reviewing the paperwork and signing the title papers and noticed an interesting fact. The parcel was subdivided in 1951 ... the year I was born. My belief is that in numbers lies a lot of truths ... and to me, this unique, tiny little fact resonated. I was indeed home ... now they will know where to find me ... if 'they' go looking ... :)

16

November's Near Miss ...

It was something out of a movie ... like yesterday was forty years ago, and today was like a distant memory. The smiles on everyone's faces were infectious ... the more everyone smiled, the harder it was not to smile. I cannot remember when two million people came together at the same moment, hugged each other, and rejoiced in the feeling of happiness that washed over their collective presence.

Hindsight is something we never think about until careful reflection. As I look back on the moment, the gathering included white middle-class kids and young adults whose only concern was leaving their natural state of mind for a moment of musical euphoria. I did not attend Woodstock, but I remember reading about it later. Half a million people converged in one place and spent the weekend together. Nothing happened, no one was hurt, and zero violence. That was news for sure ...

it would have been an incredible story to add to this book.

What happened yesterday was a celebration of love for the possibility of change. Young and old alike, of every color and creed, were smashed together as they writhed in unison. Somehow, the improbable was taking place. A black man was becoming the leader of the free world, and he offered up hope that had not been available before ... ever before.

I watched the TV and cried over his words. I felt his gratitude and mutual love for the people in the crowd. These were the real people. They were not the greedy, untrusting, untrustworthy ones he would later have to dance within the political backrooms of the world. His confidence reminded me of someone who had no idea he could fail and, likewise, no idea how to succeed. As he smiled with everyone who cried and sang his name, he too felt the overwhelming moment that just could not happen ... and yet it did.

The power of his appearance held the world's stage. His words moved the emotions of those who hated blindly, causing them to bend their knees for acceptance. Those who could not see the light drifted into the darkness alone. Yet, there was no hate for them;

instead, the hands of brotherhood invited them back into the light.

Perhaps none of this actually happened or never will. Maybe these feelings of the old 'momentary pause' in the 60s were all a dream that only a few shared. But hopefully, when we all wake up, the world will not be back to its old tricks and slavery. Believing for just a few hours might change the price of admission.

Maybe it's time we call for help sharing light so maybe our world can find eternal peace. At the end of the tunnel, the universe is waiting with open arms. Good night, all you old hippies. May the inner peace of years ago creep back into your hearts.

Freedom ...

Riding a motorcycle is truly freedom, if you know what I mean. However, at one time in my life, that statement did not mean anything. In fact, my first ride was a Honda 305 Scrambler. Imagine, I rode it barefoot and helmetless. Then, my ride moved up to a 650 BSA Spitfire. It was loud and fast, but not my favorite. I rode three-wheelers and bikes in the desert, sometimes even barefoot and almost always without a helmet. But then, I got married and had a kid. I put a helmet on, bought the kid a three-wheeler and a helmet, and finally gave up and sold everything. After which, I got sober. The lifestyle didn't fit.

Years later, a friend bought a motorcycle dealership. So, we went to the open house and laughed a little. A short time later, I bought a bike. The purchase woke my long-lost love affair. A passion that actually brought me untold happiness. I've always had gasoline in my veins. I will (for the time being) skip the iteration and get right to the present. It took many years, but I finally owned a Harley. I admit the freedom that flowed through your veins when leaving for a bike run is unexplainable.

Steve, who was in his final years on the road, was sort of fearless. If he hit a deer, he just kept driving. Now, let's not leave out Sammy, who was indeed fearless and scary all mixed up. No one pissed off Sammy. He might kick you off the bike!

Then we had Monty, the BMW man, and Fred (fat fucking freaky Fred), and all the others I met on the road. As an example, I met this big guy in the desert who always rode with weapons. But he never believed in banks and such, so he'd always stop at this property in the middle of nowhere to literally 'dig' up some cash.

On one trip, I pulled into this junction and decided to just lay back on the seat and rest my head on the handlebars. The clear, blue, sunny sky beckoned me. Once I was gone on my own, the world needed to wait on me.

The warm sun and cool breeze made me realize just how special it is to be alive. Later, a group of strangers stopped, "Do you want to ride with us?"

"No, not today, but thanks for the offer." I actually preferred to ride alone.

Then, my luck changed; I met Darma. We started riding together on my Harley retro Springer. Once the correct seat, sissy bar, footrests, and bags were attached, it was the perfect ride.

One morning, we left San Francisco and headed to the rally in Reno. Neither of us had been there before, so we chose a highway that went over the mountains and found our way. But the next morning, the weather was ugly, and I figured we'd spend the day playing slots in the casino.

However, Darma said. "We came to ride; let's go."

I said, "We're gonna get wet."

"Cool."

Well, needless to say, we rode into a huge storm and had to duck under an overpass to escape the hail. It was a complete rush ... we were soaked and laughing. Across the road, some other people were waiting out the rain as well.

I walked over to start a conversation, "Hey, I am new to the area and don't know anyone."

He abruptly cut me off, "Hey, my name is Steve. Now, you know someone."

We spent the rest of the night with his group. After the rain stopped, we hit all the cat houses and ended up in a little mountain town in a bar called the "Bucket of Blood."

If you think that is something, it just scratches the surface of what is out there to find when you pull off your boots and strike up a conversation. Explore a bit and live.

It is amazing how discovering your passions will drive you in ways unimaginable. I owned many kinds of bikes and rode every type known. The thing about the Harley is it comes off the showroom floor with thousands of instant friends. :)

White Men Can't Jump ... in Mexico

The next story that happened stems from a good part of my life. Once you hit forty, life gets pretty stable. I was doing well ... a nice home, two cars, two kids, and a handful of good friends. Much of my life centered on surfing; however, golf ranked pretty high as well. As a matter of fact, choosing between golf or surfing with my son took consideration. Except, the kid's mother reminded me that surfing with Bret took precedence 'cause golfing could wait until I got old.

My good friend Bruce had finally convinced me to go surfing in Baja without crowds. A great experience. On one of our 'fly' trips, we met another guy and his son and became good friends. Mel's son was fourteen, a year older than Bret and his friends. We began to make frequent trips to Baja with the boys and their friends. Occasionally, a few of the other fathers joined us, so we enjoyed several trips with them, camping on various cliffs above numerous breaks in remote areas far from civilization.

Once, my boss joined us and brought his fiberglass dune buggy. He was fine with the boys driving it, which surprised me. But more shocking, my comfort in letting them drive the buggy. I would watch them throw their little shortboards in the back and climb aboard for a trip down the beach. I thought, what a trip, what a good experience for them and for us.

We camped several times at the north end of a place the gringos call Long Beach. It was long, alright. We camped right where it ended and bent into a rocky point. Usually, we scored tons of waves and rarely saw anyone. During one of our trips, I noticed some land for sale and suggested we buy the property and build some A-Frame log cabins with fake snow on their roofs and rent them to surfers. No one else thought that was funny but me!!!

One evening, after we finished BBQing and cleaning up, Mel suggested that we make some popcorn and get drinks together for an after-dinner chill. So, as we worked on that project, he went to his truck and retrieved a milk carton case, a marine deep cycle battery, and a small TV with a built-in VCR. In a few minutes, Mel had the movie queued up ... we grabbed our beach chairs and lined them up in rows like a theater. Once we were all settled, drinks and snacks in arm's reach, Mel started the movie.

We sat there on a cliff with the ocean sounds in the now nearly settled sun and watched '*White Men Can't Jump.*' It was a truly magical moment as we all realized how nice it was to be alive on that beach, enjoying what we enjoyed doing. I believe that the boys had that moment of clarity, too, and though none of them are close all these years later, I am sure they glance back at that moment in their lives and smile deep down inside. :)

Political Rant … Why Not?

It was a lovely Friday morning, a holiday, and I did not know which shirt to wear to work today. But I know what I believe and what makes me say, what the F! I am going to sit and cruise through the paper. Why do I buy it? Who knows?

Anyway, a small headline caught my eye, and my jaw dropped to the floor. I felt like a child in kindergarten who somehow has the wisdom of the world, and the teacher is telling me something that does not make any sense. I admit to not reading the article. Nope, didn't even turn to it. I just read the headline and knew immediately there could be no other answers or explanations than greed, continued lies, extortion in Washington, fine cigars, expensive brandy, fast cars, huge houses, huge egos, lost time that we don't currently have to lose, dead people, more dead people, corrupt governments, more corrupt government, trickle-up economics, a coming feudal system, serfdom redefined, a one world government, loss of individuality, loss of friendships, loss of family, incredible lack of understanding that we are not stupid, a realization that much of the world has been pressed into stupidity by centuries of rules enforced by fear, understanding that religion is not spiritual, further understanding that spirituality is feared by those who rule with fear, fatigue from too many years of participating in all of the above.

Wisdom in knowing, I cannot stand in its way. Courage to at least own my truth, willingness to be ridiculed for speaking at all, loving the solitary experiences on this earth, cherishing the moments that are spent with like thinkers and lovers ... and so forth.

What was the headline, you ask? Be prepared to feel everything I just ranted. Here you go, courtesy of the San Francisco Chronicle, and I quote ... word for word—"Jets for Saudis: U.S. to sell $30 Billion worth of weaponry to the Kingdom."

Please note a couple of key ingredients in this headline. That is BILLION ... 30 BILLION ... Dollars! I know that the dollar ain't what it used to be, but that is a lot of zeros in front of the decimal point and means a lot of firepower going their way, including everything I mentioned above, going to those I referred to above. And the word that actually sparked this whole rant was 'Kingdom.' Really?

Fuckking Kingdom? Are you f#@$king kidding me? Whose Kingdom? It's a play-pen for self anointed 'Kings' we have created with our greed.

OK ... I'm exhausted, and I'm going to turn to the sports page now and pretend I never wrote this. Have a wonderful New Year and a great end to the Mayan Calendar ... Thomas Wrongshit.

17

First Time In

Early one morning, Bruce and I went surfing. After we finished, I asked, "Do you want to go to Mexico next weekend?"

"No."

"Why not?"

"I am going to hike the Grand Canyon."

"Really... can I go."

"Hell, yes."

"Cool."

Then we discussed my outfit and items needed. So, I had to make a quick trip to REI.

Bruce suggested I wear layers, he called them thermal underwear, fleece lining, and a rain shell. We went through the food and water, and I began putting my gear together.

However, I soon learned that packing is an art. Before long, I was unpacking more than packing. It was the epitome of putting ten pounds in a five-pound bag.

But alas, I was prepared to depart in the morning. We drove Bruce's wife's Bronco from Southern California to a designated meeting point at an isolated spot on the south rim of the Grand Canyon. The trip took all day to find the dirt-access road. But what I remember vividly was the total destruction of the paint on the Bronco. The deeper we went, the narrower the trail became until you could hear the limbs scoring the metal below the paint. Although, even the detailing afterward did not rub out the scratches. As I vaguely recall, Bruce sold the truck the next week and bought his wife, DeeDee, a brand-new . Corvette!

We met up with a large group who were very experienced hikers. Once everyone gathered together, we managed to set up camp before nightfall. By this time, I started to make some friends.

At dawn, we had to scramble, putting our ten pounds into the five-pound packs. Once everyone ate, we met briefly to discuss the route. Apparently, it was an unmarked access from the rim to the Esplanade level (the Esplanade is a ledge of varying width between the rim and the red rock that separates hikers from access to the bottom, and there are a limited number of accesses through the red rock to the bottom). The route took us on a little-known access to the Esplanade. This should have worried me!!!!

The hike started off nice; the descent was mild and there was good weather. Soon, the trail got very remote, but some of the passages were getting sort of crazy. Eventually, we emerged on a large boulder, edging a severe drop-off. You could see just how far we had to hike down.

Our 'leader' of sorts scaled carefully down the boulder and then disappeared through an obscure hole at the very edge. He popped back up and instructed everyone to form a line and begin passing packs down to him. As they arrived, he lowered them on a rope to a spot we could not see yet. One pack actually rolled off the ledge, and we were able to retrieve it later. And then, one by one, we all inched our way to the ledge and slipped through the hole. What we discovered upon entry to the hole was a tree that had been stripped and its limbs to create a ladder down. It was probably twenty to thirty feet, as I recall.

When everyone landed safely, we shouldered our packs and carefully negotiated a very narrow trail that traversed the mountain immediately below the boulder. Eventually, we came to a razorback to use as an access to the Esplanade below. Just finding this route was amazing, but finding it on my first trip ever was crazy. The Arizona climbers (who had made at least ten previous trips down) had read about this trail and actually visited the author to discuss it with him. We were off the grid for sure.

However, no matter how cool the trip, you had to ruin your vehicle getting to the trailhead. Or, spend days trimming branches. But that evening was a hoot at camp. Most of the group took a sigh of relief that the trek down was completed. Nevertheless, we speculated about the hike. By the way, it was the only way out!!

The next day was full of day hikes, and I met my first scary moment and was forced to turn back. These guys were climbing over a huge boulder in the path and landing on the other side. It was too narrow a landing point for me, and the fall was several hundred feet below. Death ... I was not the only one who turned back either. But the worst part of the whole trip was the lack of two very important commodities that Bruce forgot to mention ... really?

I had no chocolate, sugar of some sort, or coffee. No fucking coffee! Really? All around me were M&Ms and coffee. But the golden rule was carrying your own stuff. And asking for something that someone else carried was a no-no. And being a sport, I did not ask for anything ... almost.

We stopped to rest that afternoon, and my willpower failed. I asked this guy, "Hey, can I have a few M&Ms?"

"Sure ..." I woofed them down in record time.

Then he opened a jar of fish eggs, "Would you like some of these too?"

"Uhhh, no thanks."

He laughed and shoved another bite in his mouth. These were nice people and good friends. The same guy made a pot of cowboy coffee in the morning, and I almost cried as I drank my cup. :)

The next day was a reverse of the downward trip, and although it was challenging (to say the least), we all made it back to the cars. I did enjoy this trip. It was far from what I expected, and every bit was what I expected. Three of the other guys agreed that they would meet up again soon and make a trip to the bottom. Was I in? Hell, yes ... I'm in!!! What bottom?

I Might be Bald, But I'm Still Alive

We left early on a Thursday morning to rally the troops. However, it was a long time ago, so some of the names have escaped me. On a four-day outing to 'Seven Sisters' in Baja about halfway to Cabo, I rode with Mel, who brought only one CD. What band do you ask? The *Beach Boys Greatest Hits* of course! And in the middle of nowhere, we only had two radio channels.

What were you thinking? Ten hours on the road with only fourteen songs. And it had to be the Beach Boys. If I was stranded on a desert island, that would have been the last of my choices.

After a couple of miles, Mel says, "Do you hear that repetitive banging?"

"Yep."

So, he rolls down the window. Suddenly, the burning rubber rolls inside the cab. Needless to say, once we got out, the problem became crystal clear. The right rear tire was destroyed. When our other party caught up and got out, they started laughing.

We were a long way from anywhere and from a Firestone store, and we were in a hurry to find waves. So, we unloaded the back of the jeep, fished out the spare tire (luckily a full-size spare), laced it up, and off we went.

But we got another shock when we reached 'Zippers.' It was small and very crowded. How could that be? Crowded this far down … so, we headed north towards 'Seven Sisters'.

The name referred to seven similar points jutting out with a northern exposure. The road north along the coast was rugged and slow going. Eventually, we came to a small town (or village, if you like), and it had a tire store. The man at the shop was friendly.

I rolled the destroyed tire out and asked, "Do you think it can be fixed?" He did not understand the humor! "Just kidding. Do you have a tire we can buy?"

He smiled and mounted an old tire … good enough for a spare. Plus, we got gas … well kinda. We took turns siphoning gas through a long hose from large cans balanced on the top of a step ladder. Crude but efficient!

Finally, all the problems were mended, so we headed north to the waves. Then we stumbled onto another slightly larger town in the middle of nowhere and pushed through it to the north side. We found a lined-up pointbreak with glassy waves pumping and no one riding them.

When we got close to the gate, and since there was no evidence of recent camping on the sandy point, Bruce, who spoke simple Spanish, said, "Sit tight. I'll go to town and see what's up with the point and why it has electronics out at the end."

We played guitars, enjoyed the sun, and talked excitedly about the waves. Bruce returned with the low down. The little town was raising abalone in a huge warehouse and then planting them in the bay just south of the point. After they matured and were harvested, Taiwanese investors shipped them home. I guess abalone is a huge delicacy in Taiwan.

Bruce relayed Senior Esteban's premonition, "We could camp and surf, but we could not dive or fish. But watch for drug smugglers who often tried to steal the abalone on their way south. So, the town had vigilantes that patrolled the point at night." He continued, "If anyone came into our camp, not to worry; just tell them that Senior Esteban said it was cool to be there."

On the first night, two large men carrying very large guns walked into our camp and just looked at us. Claude and I were playing guitars and everyone else was in their tents asleep.

So, Claude smiles, "Mariachis!" They did not smile.

About that time, Bruce poked his head out and mentioned Senior Esteban and the two turned and walked back into the darkness.

We had a great time, surfed a lot, and thought we saw sharks swimming around us that turned out to be Manna Rays. We met the local kids and gave them surf magazines and the clothes we always brought to give the locals.

They loved us and brought food, then invited us to town on Sunday for their weekend baseball game against a neighboring town.

Bruce and I went to the game, and it was cool. We were welcomed by most and protected from the hecklers by these new friends, and yes, we paid to get in like everyone else. They drank beer from large troughs of ice and had a great afternoon. It was a very cultural experience, and I will never forget the feeling of being among total strangers, mostly drunk strangers, and still feeling quite at home and safe.

Claude, one of the group members, decided on the final night to have his buddy shave his head. So, after drinking enough tequila to kill a horse, his buddy butchered his hair with battery-powered clippers and a small pair of scissors. But that did not stop Claude from saucing it up more. Before long, he was rowdy, falling every time he got up.

The group decided the best option was to get him back to the tent and to sleep.

However, the plan failed when he raced out of this tent, slurring, "Man is drawn to fire." A famous Bevis and Butthead line, "I need more teepee for my bunghole."

Finally, he passed out, and we laid him face down in the middle of the crowd so he wouldn't choke.

The next morning, sometime in the early morning, he made it back to his tent and passed out. We'd all decided to catch some waves but stopped to check in on him beforehand.

He unzipped the window and saw daylight, "Man, you are messed up. You look like a mental patient."

An absolute mess; his eyes were bloodshot and half closed, not to mention his hair. "Well, I might be bald, but I'm still alive!!"

We all agreed he might have to be smuggled in a trunk back into the US. Claude was half German and half Hawaiian and looked like a Mexican who had escaped from the nut house. :) We made it home, and his wife hated his hair ... go figure!!!

Didn't See That Coming

It was a sunny morning on the Baja Peninsula, and we were camped at the north end of a place the locals called Long Beach. We really liked this place. It was about two hours south of Ensenada, just past the tennis courts, right at the church in a small town called … well I can't tell you, or I'd have to kill you. :)

Either way, it was a scenic drive through Rancho and down to the ocean. An adventurous drive.

Our first trip, Bruce and I were heading through Rancho when we stopped a local ranch hand and asked, "Are we heading in the right direction?"

"Yes, but you'd better hurry?"

"Why?"

He smiled, "You're on the Baja 500 Race Track, and they're on their way."

"What the fuck?!"

We loaded up and hauled ass south along the coast and found the place we knew and loved. The camp was just off the road, at a ninety-degree left turn. A perfect place, we had a ditch between us and the road on an elbow turn, with the ocean to our backs.

Since the coast was clear, we decided to surf before dark. But as we started cooking dinner, the motorcycles came roaring up in the distance. It was a two-stroke wound out heading our way. In a few short minutes, this green 250 cc Kawi dove into the corner, jammed the accelerator and blew by us in a flash. He was close, but the ditch served as protection. For the next several hours, we lay under the stars and listened to the nonstop parade of motorcycles, jeeps, trucks, and buggies fly into that corner and race off over the hill and out of sight and sound. It was exciting.

Another time, we were coasting along through Rancho, heading down to the ocean, when we made the left bend at the ocean and noticed a little house down the slope right on the water. We'd seen it before, but it was different. There were two or three stretch black limos parked in front.

Wait, this was a poor section of the Baja, so only one option left: federals or politicians. Either way, we did the Mexico thing and minded our own business. We didn't even pause for a look. But, don't think for a second, we did not have our heads on a swivel.

18

The Rune Palace

I was heading to Burning Man for the second time. Just so there is no misunderstanding about the "theme" for the 2004 event, which factors into this story, is copied in the text below.

On my second trip to Burning Man, the art theme happened to be *Vault of Heaven,* illustrated by Rod Garrett.

The "theme" usually drives most of the art displays. As at the previous year (my first trip to Burning Man) complete strangers who camped across the street became great friends. A typical playa experience. They introduced me to the Nordic Rune Stones of (and this is what I was told ... not researched) the sixth century B.C. The symbols on these stones, twenty-five pieces total if you count the "blank" Rune (the alpha and the omega), are recognizable in many modern-day symbols today.

The stones are not used in fortune telling; they actually represent certain times and phases of life. When pulled randomly, they have an uncanny ability to link with your mental state, symbolizing your life at the moment. The accuracy is spooky.

About six months before the event, I decided the Runes were going to be in my "theme" camp contribution. In my mind's eye, I visualized a four-sided room with a door size opening at every corner ... each facing toward a compass direction. With that thought in place, I began gathering rocks in the low deserts of Southern California.

The problem was finding 5,000 flat (enough) stones of a similar size needed to make 200 complete sets. The idea behind the Rune Palace was to come inside, relax, and experience a reading. You would be encouraged to pick twenty-five stones and markers to imprint symbols on the stones. Then, you'd receive a sheet with the readings that applied to each stone and a small bag for taking them home.

While hiking in the desert with two friends who did not understand Burning Man, I began picking up small rocks. They were interested in why but laughed out loud after my explanation.

A couple of weeks later, I rolled into my trailer hideaway and found a handful of perfectly round (nearly) flat stones on my porch with a note describing briefly where the fellow hiker had run into them. Sandy even tied her scarf to a nearby bush to mark the spot. I pulled my four-wheeler out of the trailer and prepared to head out on the hunt. Sandy stopped by that afternoon and went with me. The find ended up being off the map wild.

I have no idea how she stumbled upon this find, but there were hundreds, no thousands of these stones everywhere. They were strewn across a sand-covered hill in the middle of the desert. I was amazed.

I researched them later that evening, and Google suggested the stones to be between 5,000- and 10,000-year-old sandstone balls unearthed in a flood decade, maybe centuries ago, and left exposed to the harsh daily desert sun. Eventually, they began to split apart into wafers.

I found many already lying flat and others still looking like a ball until touched. These stones were absolutely perfect for my project, but the way I arrived at their existence was serendipitous to the 10th degree!

Needless to say, over a short period, I returned several times and hand-carried thousands. The action did not leave me without trepidation. Some people thought the rock should stay in their natural habitat; others did not see a problem.

In the end, the Burning Man event would transport them into many homes in the world. So, if you get the Rune thing, these stones are very connected to the earth.

Brown Liquor and Sting Ray Bikes

My summer between the eighth and ninth grades was a hard one. The local boys and I spent a lot of time cruising the beach on our Sting Ray bikes. We could ride them on the back wheel for what seemed like ever, maneuver through tight spots and cars, carry our belly boards and fins, plus ditch just about anyone. A very brief moment of my life spent on a bike.

We were not the most behaved group of early teenage boys—in essence, the un-parented contingency. When we graduated from junior high, the school set up chairs and organized a small graduation ceremony on the PE field. I remember it like it was yesterday.

On the field were the proud parents of most of the students. And then there was us. We were hanging around on the fringe on our bikes. School was out, none of our parents were attending, and participating seemed pointless. But we hung out and watched. It never occurred to me not partaking was strange ... it just was.

Our small group was destined to get into big trouble that summer. There might have been more, but the core group remained small. Some of us were thieves however, we all sort of went along with the thief leaders on occasion. The usual escapades included sneaking into theaters, drinking under the bridge, playing pool, and trouble in general. There was nothing family about the Family Billiards place either.

The young men in our group pushed the limit ... often. I remember New Year's Eve 1964/65. Somehow, the three of us were free for the night. No parents asking where, why or when ... so off we went on our bikes. We followed Ron to his grandmother's trailer on the bay. She was gone, so we climbed through a window, found a brand-new bottle of VO, opened it, and began chugging one after the other.

Mark stopped first because he was smarter, I guess. Ron and I kept on but split pretty soon. We shoved the bottle back into the cupboard, almost empty, and left. It was time to get an early dinner on the peninsula at a place called the Blue Dolphin.

However, just getting there was a miracle. The brown liquor took hold rapidly and riding without falling was becoming a problem. Somehow, we made our destination, which was quite a trek and required crossing some major roads. Although riding took a toll, walking was another story. I excused myself and went to the bathroom because things started spinning, and I had to sit down. The VO turned against me, and I got ill.

316

In the stall heaving, a stranger walked in, "Oh My God."

In my mind, the end was near...I did not know anything about alcohol poisoning, but I could not get caught.

The incident scared me so bad I left the restaurant, grabbed my bike, and staggered to the end of the building. Around the corner were some bushes to stash the bike out of sight and hide till dawn. It might have been about 5 pm, and to this day, I have no idea what happened to Ron and Mark.

I woke up covered in puke, wet, and freezing. It was still dark, so I figured it was time to get out and stay out of sight. I had survived alcohol poisoning but had to get home without getting busted for curfew.

Back then, the curfew for minors was 10 pm, and the police called your parents to come and get you. As I mentioned earlier, we were all skilled with our Sting Ray bikes. I stealthily skimmed along the dark roads and, like a bad penny, was shortly walking through the front door of our apartment. Juanita was sitting up waiting for me, she was supposed to be out all night.

The morale ... Juanita was pissed! I smelled like Bourbon and vomit. She threw me in the shower, clothes and all, then berated me for my stupidity. After which, I went to bed with a headache, very hungry and thirsty. Wanna know what the next morning was like? Guess ... cause, I have no recollection ... but I assume it was just another day in the life with Juanita Odessa.

XMAS Prayer Song

Our Father, which art in Heaven

Hallowed be thy name

Thy kingdom come, thy will be done

On earth as it is in heaven

Give us this day our daily bread

Forgive us our trespasses as we

Forgive those who trespass against us

Lead us not into temptation

But deliver us from Evil

For thine is the Kingdom, the Power

And the glory forever ... Amen

God grant me the serenity to accept the

thing I cannot charge

The courage to change the things I can

And the wisdom to know the difference

I pray for the knowledge of your will for me today

And ability to listen

Every day, I am getting better and better and better

My improvement is for the improvement of mankind

I am in control of my faculties and my sensing devices
Including my outer sensing devices
I will always remember that only positive images
will bring to me things that I desire

Square Pegism

The saying, 'Square Pegs in Round Holes,' defines me to a tee. Sometimes, I sit next to the round holes, and other times I put a corner in them and sort of rest—kind of in the hole.

In no way could I ever understand becoming a square peg. The round holes are fine, round, and happy. However, some round holes are nice, while others resent my square shape. So, I always give the resentful ones the right-of-way ... after all, I am the square peg ... not them.

Yet, sometimes, the round holes are beyond my comprehension, and I lose touch with my square pegism. It is then that I find the only moments that allow me to feel uncomfortable and able to touch my inner feelings.

As a square peg, I rarely react and almost never, never cry. I could not deal with the round holes that see my tears. So, because I am a square peg, I smile instead and permit the round holes to move to their own music. And once in a while, I cry myself to sleep. And then I dream of a life with square pegs.

Printed in the USA
CPSIA information can be obtained
at www.ICGtesting.com
CBHW070246020524
7838CB00008B/89

9 781648 734908